SAGE CONTEMPORARY SOCIAL SCIENCE ISSUES 19

S0-CJQ-017

THE

FEMALE

OFFENDER

Edited by

Annette M. Brodsky

Ⓢ **SAGE** PUBLICATIONS *Beverly Hills / London* 1975

HV6046
F37

The material in this publication originally appeared as a special issue of CRIMI-NAL JUSTICE AND BEHAVIOR (Volume 1, Number 4, December 1974). The Publisher would like to acknowledge the assistance of the special issue editor, Annette M. Brodsky, in making this edition possible.

For information address:

SAGE PUBLICATIONS, INC.
275 South Beverly Drive
Beverly Hills, California 90212

SAGE PUBLICATIONS LTD
St George's House / 44 Hatton Garden
London EC1N 8ER

Printed in the United States of America

International Standard Book Number 0-8039-0568-8

Library of Congress Catalog Card No. 75-27014

FIRST PRINTING (this edition)

CONTENTS

00633

THE FEMALE OFFENDER

EDITOR'S INTRODUCTION

This special issue of *Criminal Justice and Behavior* addresses itself to the female offender. There is an awakening interest in women as a subgroup of the criminal justice system, partly because of the rising crime rate among women and the increasing numbers of females in penal institutions. The "forgotten offender" has been the focus of a new flurry of attention. As researchers, correctional administrators, and law enforcement personnel become confronted with the change in behavior of women in relation to crime, there is a need for organizing the available knowledge about this population and fostering the continuing investigation of problems they cause and the difficulties they experience.

This issue is divided into two sections: the first part deals with an empirical approach to the study of female offenders. The investigation of the female experience in the correctional literature by Christine Rasche suggests that history repeats itself in the cycles of feminism, rise in female crime, and resulting focus on the woman as criminal. The articles by Panton on sex differences of prison inmates on a personality inventory and by Cavior et al. on the role of attractiveness in female offenders provide new insights into the accumulating literature on causation and dynamics of the female offender population. Michaud's bibliography offers resource to the researcher through a thoughtful and wide-ranging documentation of the literature concerning adult female offenders. This bibliography should help to remedy the paucity of background data reported by investigators in this subject area.

The second section of this volume is drawn from the papers and proceedings of the Third Alabama Symposium on Justice and the Behavioral Sciences held in January 1974. The title of the symposium was "Planning for the Female Offender," and the goals and nature of the symposium reports are described in the introduction to the section.

I am very grateful to several individuals for their contributions to this special issue. My appreciation is extended to the authors who submitted articles, and those who provided references to workers in the field who are dealing with female offenders. The readers of manuscripts provided valuable critiques and much time and effort. Special thanks are extended to Stanley Brodsky, editor of *Criminal Justice and Behavior,* for his willingness to support a special issue devoted to female offenders and his editorial help in the many guidelines, problems, and procedures that confront a guest editor.

—Annette M. Brodsky

THE FEMALE OFFENDER AS AN OBJECT OF CRIMINOLOGICAL RESEARCH

CHRISTINE E. RASCHE
Sociology Department
University of North Florida

The historical development of research approaches toward the etiology of female crimes and the characteristics of female offenders is traced through the correctional literature of the last century. The changes of theories and focus of research are related to the changes in general attitudes toward women over this period. The current status of the literature indicates that the female offender is changing along with the role of women in society. Criminological knowledge of the female offender is incomplete in many areas and increasingly obsolete. Those studies based on male populations are of untested validity for women.

"The special problems of the delinquent woman have at all times been neglected—or glossed over by sentiment and unreliable male intuition." So wrote Ann Smith in 1965, neatly summing up the conclusions of all who have looked at the scientific literature on the female offender. The vast bulk of criminological research, unquestionably, has concerned itself with male offenders and male correctional institutions or treatment programs with male participants. We can—and must— legitimately question whether findings from these studies are generalizable to female offenders. In fact, two studies of correctional institutions for females each showed that many aspects of the inmate social system described by previous researchers were not present at all or to the same degree in female facilities as they were in male institutions, because such social structures were essentially the products of male psychology. The peculiarities of inmate social structure in female institutions, by contrast, can be seen to reflect the psychological needs of women in our culture (Giallombardo, 1966; Ward and Kassebaum, 1965). Under these circumstances, it is valid to ask whether many other of our criminological findings are not similarly specific only to male offenders.

It is perhaps surprising that criminological research should have been so confined to male offenders since women's reformatories were among the very first to involve themselves in research. The Bedford Hills Reformatory for Women in New York engaged its own psychologist in 1910 and opened a Laboratory of Social Hygiene for the purpose of research in 1912. A Massachusetts reformatory for women established a research department at about the same time, well ahead of similar developments in male institutions in these or other states (Lekkerkerker, 1931). But most of these early pioneering efforts at research were short-lived due to insufficient financial support and official apathy. Thereafter, when research was instituted, it almost universally took its samples from male institutions, and female populations were neglected.

There are many reasons for this consistent neglect. The first and most primary is that women comprise less than 5% of the entire prison population in the United States—there simply aren't as many female prisoners as there are male. The 1970 census data on inmates of institutions established that there were only 13,451 women in federal, state, and local jails and prisons, compared to 304,389 men. Over half of these women were in jails (presumably on lesser charges) while almost two-thirds of the men were in state and federal prisons (presumably on greater charges). Furthermore, women are not even arrested as often as men; in 1972, according to FBI Uniform Crime Reports, male arrests outnumbered female arrests by almost six to one. Because of their relative smallness in numbers, women offenders are frequently considered to be mere "complications" in general data collecting. Thus, the Task Force Report on Corrections by the President's Commission on

Law Enforcement and the Administration of Justice did not devote even a single paragraph to female offenders, considering it sufficient to acknowledge that the correctional institution population is 95% male and that males and females have different patterns of employment, for example, which would affect general data substantially.

Small populations of female offenders mean that researchers interested in them will have fewer subjects for study, complicating statistical findings and, of course, lowering the generalizability of the data. As Smith (1962) has noted, those who have studied female offenders often disagree as to the importance of factors such as age or social status upon women offenders, usually because their research was forced to rely on small numbers and took place in vastly different settings.

Because there are substantially fewer women arrested or imprisoned, there are substantially fewer women involved in rehabilitation programs. New or experimental programs often receive research attention and/or publication, and it is typical that women are neglected in these areas. Even if women were involved in treatment programs proportionately to their numbers, they would still constitute a very small group. But there is evidence to suggest that, especially at the state and local levels, experimental programs are initiated among male inmates and, if they are successful there, then expanded to the female inmates, if at all. This is true, for example, in Missouri, where adult male prisoners who receive parole are processed through a 30-day prerelease program prior to leaving the prison. No such program exists for the female releasees because not enough women are released each month to "warrant" one. Even federal programs are not exempt from this tendency: of 4,000 offenders who received job training under the Manpower Development and Training Act by June 1970, only 143 were women. Consequently, female offenders not only receive less research attention, they receive less rehabilitation attention, and our lack of knowledge about them is perpetuated.

Besides their small numbers, there are several other reasons for the relatively meager scientific data on female offenders.

Smith (1962) observes that, at least in England, inquiries into the case histories and other particulars of imprisoned women are more frequently opposed by both correctional officials and the women themselves than are those of males. Even the "fallen" woman must have what is left of her virtue protected.

Blos (1969) has speculated that the study of female sexual delinquency, as a particular type of offense, has been forfeited either because of its "taboo and socially embarrassing aspects" or because "our society as a whole may be somewhat more ambivalent about its desire to terminate sexually promiscuous behavior in girls than it is about its desire to terminate the destructive behavior of delinquent boys, directed against property and other persons." Indeed, there is ample reason for concluding that much of female criminality has been unexplored primarily because it has been viewed as essentially nondangerous to other persons—socially offensive rather than actually dangerous.

There is at least one other reason for the lack of research attention to female offenders: women themselves have been disregarded as important or as fit topics of research. It is perhaps significant that all of the pioneering research, as at the Bedford Hills Reformatory, was initiated, conducted, and reported by female researchers, and that the bulk of scientific data on female offenders to date has been unearthed by female investigators. There are important exceptions to this, of course; some of the most distinctive and/or significant studies of female offenders have been done by men such as Lombroso, Pollak, Ward, and Kassebaum. In general, however, male researchers have studied male offenders, and until recently there have not been very many female researchers. One famous criminologist who teaches at a major university remarked that he can never get his male graduate students to pick up this neglected area because "it is less attractive to them," and the few female graduate students he receives "usually end up in juvenile delinquency or other familial areas."

This avoidance of female criminality as a research area has given support to advocates of women's liberation, who see this as just another symptom of the status of women in an unequal society. The conspicuous lack of scientific information on women offenders is simply another indication to many observers that women, even when they get in trouble with the law, are less important than men. Thus, Burkhart (1971) charges that "To have spent time in a women's joint is to fully appreciate the status of women in 20th century America," and that it is because "so little thought has been given to them that information on women behind bars is almost nonexistent."

Because what literature which exists on female criminality is almost completely buried in technical professional journals or larger studies of male offenders, even existing knowledge is not widely dispersed. Therefore, while "meager" to the trained social scientist, it is truly "nonexistent" to the layman, who is then left to rely solely upon newspaper, television, movie, and magazine accounts for his or her information. Unfortunately, there is frequently a tendency in the media, in the absence of factual information, to get exotic on the subject. Women in prison thus come to be portrayed either as tigresses, wild and passionately possessed, or as virtually innocent victims of cruel and sadistic keepers. Women's institutions are often portrayed as exact replicas of the worst male prisons with tiers of cells and lockstep rules, or dungeon-like corridors of cages. This tendency to emphasize the physically brutal or seductive aspects of prison life and to picture female prisoners exotically is similar in many regards to the ways in which females are described and made to act in pornographic literature. In their study of sexual imagination, Drs. Phyllis and Eberhard Kronhausen (1969) have asserted that much of the erotic fantasy literature, written by and for men, ascribes to women the attitudes and behaviors men think women have. Consequently, though the literature "abounds in descriptions of female homosexuality," these stories "do not reflect the true feelings of female homosexuals nor are they descriptive of lesbian attitudes or sexual practices." Likewise, many pulp magazines and movies offer stories of women in prison which sound like they were composed by someone with only a passing knowledge of the subject but a very creative imagination. This is not to say that such conditions of incarceration might not exist; it is only to assert that they are certainly the exception rather than the rule. The problems with prisons, and with women in prisons, are deeper, more subtle, and more resistant to change than these depictions would suggest.

There is a great need, therefore, to clarify some of the popular misconceptions which have arisen in the absence of scientific data, but there are also other reasons for paying new attention to female criminality. One reason is that the arrest rate for females is increasing faster than that for males, and more females are being brought into court and sentenced to prison terms than was true previously. According to FBI statistics (Uniform Crime Reports, 1973), in the five years between 1967 and 1972 the arrest rate for men increased 18%, while for women it increased 72%, mostly because of a large increase in the arrest of women for larcenies. More young girls are appearing in juvenile court nationwide, with crimes involving girls increasing twice as fast as those involving boys in 1969 and 1970. In short, though still in the minority, the number of females coming in contact with the criminal justice system and being sent to prison is growing larger. If this trend continues, many women's institutions, built to accommodate small numbers, will need expansion or new quarters. The possibility of incorporating progressive treatment programs into these facilities will depend upon availability of scientific data to a large extent. Furthermore, there is the generally overlooked consideration that female criminality may be in many regards an "iceberg problem." That is to say, the criminality of women which becomes known is but a minority proportion of that which exists below the surface, and its most serious aspect may be that of its far-reaching consequences—i.e., its effect upon children, both those remaining with and separated from their lawbreaking mothers. There is a need for research which will clarify the influence of female criminality upon the total criminal scene, where it may have large, unexplored implications.

Although the literature on female offenders has been comparatively limited, studies have been done and, in fact, the development of the study of female offenders reflects the larger development of the study of criminal behavior in general. That is to say, the study of female criminality, when traced historically, can be seen to mirror the phases through which the general study of criminology has passed. A look at these phases reveals that the study of crime and criminals, including females, has gone through at least five major stages of development, each characterized by a particular type of focus.

STAGES IN THE CRIMINOLOGICAL STUDY OF THE FEMALE OFFENDER

The first stage can be called the *prescientific* stage, and it encompasses almost everything written on the subject of crime up to the start of the twentieth century. As far as female offenders are concerned, that includes virtually nothing. Women were then, as now, such a minute portion of the deviant element that little was set forth on them specifically. Certainly, notorious females received popular attention, but almost nothing specific to women is to be found in the ethical and theoretical treatises on crime, and its causes and prevention, which dominate the prescientific period. The few references made about women in this regard show clearly that women were generally considered morally corrupt (as opposed to evil) when they transgressed the law, but were not taken seriously as a danger to society. Hence the terms "fallen" or "errant" which were so often applied to females who pursued criminal careers; women were seen as essentially virtuous unless they "fell" from their pedestals or were "led astray" by others. Very few women were labeled "evil," but when such labeling occurred, it was with a vengeance. Often, "evil" women were portrayed as supernatural, or as witches, and therefore, no longer deserving of the protection or politeness normally extended toward women.

The prescientific stage of criminology was essentially devoted to moral-ethical and armchair theorizing which resulted ultimately in the development and growth of the penitentiary system in early nineteenth-century America. The penitentiary was the product of the development of a causal theory of crime which pinpointed a corrupt environment and lax upbringing as the causes of criminal behavior. Probably the earliest specific reference to female offenders in this body of theory occurs in a 1823 Report of the Society for the Prevention of Pauperism written by the Society's founder, a Dr. Griscom, who was arguing for a proposed house of refuge. One of the categories of individuals cited by Dr. Griscom as needing the care of such a refuge was that of "delinquent females, who are either too young to have acquired habits of fixed depravity, or those whose lives have in general been virtuous, but who, having yielded to the seductive influences of corrupt associates, have suddenly to endure the bitterness of lost reputation, and are cast forlorn and destitute upon a cold and unfeeling public, full of compunction for their errors, and anxious to be restored to the paths of innocence and usefulness" (Reeves, 1929).

This sort of causal·theory may be classified as one of environmentalism. When the penitentiary idea failed, environmentalism was seriously jeopardized. One of the chief concerns of penal theorists who puzzled over the failure of the penitentiary idea was a concern for "habitual" criminal offenders, since recidivists destroyed completely the penitentiary's underlying theory. The fact that some persons should pursue criminal behavior when any "rational man" would have abandoned it led to an interest in pinpointing constitutional features which might be related to such obstinate pursuit.

The second stage of criminological research, then, involved *the search for constitutional causes,* and reflected a beginning interest in the criminal as an individual. This interest can be roughly divided into two types: interest in (1) physiological characteristics, and (2) mental characteristics. The hope of theorists at this point was that if large numbers of criminals were carefully studied, certain identifiable characteristics might emerge which would enable society to distinguish "real criminals" from those who offended "by accident." The most famous researcher of this period was Ceasar Lombroso, whose study of *The Female Offender* first appeared in 1893. Actually Lombroso had been preceded a few years before by Pauline Tarnowsky, who studied female thieves and prostitutes in Italy in an effort to find characteristics which would define "a criminal type." Both Tarnowsky and Lombroso sought physiological characteristics and followed a school of thought which involved taking elaborate cranial measurements. After a lot of painstaking and detailed work, however, Lombroso was forced to conclude that the concept of the "born criminal" which he had developed by studying male offenders was rare among women. But he went on to try to explain this finding by asserting that women were innately inferior to men morally. Thus, most women were "occasional offenders," whose latent criminal tendencies would surface when normal constraints were missing. However, when a woman *did* fall into the category of "born criminal," Lombroso asserted that she was "more terrible than the male." Because of her innate depravity, her insensitivity to pain "which breeds lack of compassion," and her childish qualities—i.e., jealousy, cruelty, revengefulness, and moral deficiency—the normal female (who was otherwise an "innocuous semi-criminal") could be transformed into a "born criminal" whose propensities for evil were "more intense and more perverse" than those of male born criminals. Moreover, the born female criminal was a double exception, since criminals were an exception among civilized people, and women criminals were "an exception among criminals," and, "as a double exception, the criminal woman is consequently a monster. Her normal sister is kept in the paths of virtue by many causes, such as maternity, piety, weakness, and when these counter influences fail, and a woman commits a crime, we may conclude that her wickedness must have been enormous before it could triumph over so many obstacles" (Lombroso, 1958).

Most of Lombroso's conclusions have been rejected today, of course. Unfortunately, however, his concept of the "born criminal" has remained in the popular mind long after it was scientifically discredited. The image of the criminal woman as the innately "bad" woman, beyond redemption, with superior powers of seduction and manipulation, remains.

Lombroso was by no means alone in his search for physiologically constitutional characteristics of female criminals. Most notably, Matthews in 1923, Burt in 1925, and Seagrave in 1926 all studied female offenders from the point of view of physical size and development, sexual development, illness, and disease; but few really outstanding causal relationships were ever uncovered (Smith, 1962). Meanwhile, however, other constitutionally oriented researchers were studying the *mental* attributes of female offenders in efforts to connect delinquency with mental aberrations or disease. The best of these studies took place at the Bedford Hills Reformatory. In 1916, Weidensall published *The Mentality of the Criminal Woman,* a report of her findings from comparative mental testing. In general she found that the criminal woman tended to be slow to comprehend instructions and thus tended to act "blindly without comprehension" instead of stopping to think matters through. With training, however, many of the women were able to learn to be quite efficient at a task; consequently, Weidensall concluded that "when one has recognized and satisfactorily explained this slow, yet really existent, ability to learn and then evaluated it in terms of their social requirements and facilities for training, the problem of how to understand and deal with the criminal woman will have been in large part solved." The task of corrections, then, would be to distinguish between those who are able to learn and those who are truly dull and would not be able to put their acquired skills to use in the outside world.

The conclusion that a large proportion of the female criminals confined in institutions were mentally deficient was supported by Spaulding in 1923 and the Gluecks in 1939. However, it soon became apparent to some researchers that the subnormal intelligence found in such studies was not necessarily related to criminality as such, but to institutionalization. After all, the smartest, most careful and alert criminals were not apprehended as often as the dull ones. Thus, the studies of constitutional characteristics became more cautious with the years. Fernald in 1920, for example, found two influences which seemed to be related to female delinquency: (1) poor economic background and lack of education or training; and (2) "a somewhat inferior mentality." However, Fernald warned that these conclusions were not tested against a normal sample and it was not known to what degree these two factors appeared within the general population. As far as the inferior mentality was concerned, "The most that we are prepared to say is that, other things being equal, there is apparently a greater presumption in favor of delinquency in a group of women who are below the average in intelligence than in a group above the average." Actually, Fernald and her associates were struck more by the *low degree* of the relationships between background and mental ability and criminal behavior than by their existence at all. In fact, they were confident that these distinctions between criminals and normals would decrease with more exhaustive study. They concluded that:

> Within all groups and all classes there are doubtless individuals whose adjustments to the demands of society are more or less precarious. Whether or not they become delinquent will depend, not so much upon the appearance of a single decisive factor, as upon the massing of factors in such a way as to disturb a more or less unstable initial adjustment. That certain factors, notably poor economic conditions, variously operative, and inferior intelligence, are particularly likely so to disturb the balance is the main point which we should urge in emphasizing these conditions.

Fernald clearly asserted a multicausal approach to crime, and by the 1930s the study of female criminals had firmly entered its third stage, in which crime was seen as a product of *both constitutional and environmental factors*. One of the most overly-discussed environmental factors in nonscientific circles was that of sexual emancipation. Thus in 1931, Cecil Bishop, a Scotland Yard veteran, observed that the crime rate was "appreciably higher" in England than it had been prior to World War I, and, according to his interpretations, women were largely responsible for this increase. It was significant to him "that the emancipation of women should have coincided so closely with a profound change in the social outlook of the community." Though he disclaimed being an anti-feminist, Bishop was no believer in equality of the sexes, and felt that the emancipation movement had resulted in (1) more women becoming "criminally-minded," (2) a "better class woman" turning criminal more often, and in (3) women being involved in sexual misdemeanors at a younger age than ever before. This voluntary involvement in criminal behavior was especially aggravating, Bishop believed, at a time when women seemed more pressed by economic or family conditions to turn to crime, as well as being more often the victims of white slavers and others who forced them into criminal behavior. Bishop's treatise was essentially nonscientific, but it reflects well the temper of the times regarding female criminality.

By far one of the most interesting studies to come from this period, however, was that of the Dutch lawyer, Eugenia Lekkerkerker, who visited the United States in the late 1920s to study female reformatories. Her report, *Reformatories for Women in the United States,* published in 1931, traced the growth of separate reformatories for women, gave lengthy descriptions of those institutions which she visited and their programs, and made some interesting observations. First, she noted that about half of all women committed to prisons or reformatories in the first six months of 1923 had been convicted of

> prostitution, fornication, adultery, disorderly conduct or vagrancy, i.e., sex offenses which in Holland would either not be punishable at all, or would rarely be punished with imprisonment.

Furthermore, where females and sexual behavior was concerned, she observed, the United States tended to merge legal and medical concerns, sending to the reformatories not all women who violated the sexual codes but particularly those suffering from venereal disease. Some jurisdictions required medical exams of all women convicted of sexual offenses, with those who were disease-free receiving probation while those who were not received imprisonment. In some cases, freedom hinged on being "cured." Lekkerkerker was quick to point out that the actions taken against women in this regard were not paralleled by similar actions against the men involved in sex offenses. Furthermore, since these tactics only affected a "negligible percentage" of all those afflicted with the disease, Lekkerkerker felt herself "inclined to agree" with those who were denouncing the practices as unfair to women.

Lekkerkerker was also one of the first to observe that women offenders were often handled with "noncriminal methods" and either granted probation, dismissed, or turned over to private agencies or supervision without any sort of formal conviction. Two factors primarily accounted for this, she believed: (1) the fact that officials hesitated to send minor offenders to the reformatory, and (2) the fact that sexual delinquency was not seriously considered a crime. In a classic statement, Lekkerkerker observed

> The fact is, that from the beginning women delinquents were much more regarded as erring and misguided human beings needing protection and help than as dangerous criminals against whom the social order should be protected. As we have noted before, the majority of the women delinquents, especially in the Massachusetts prison, had been guilty either of drunkenness or of sex delinquency, both offenses with which, as the common saying goes, "they had harmed no one but themselves." The more serious and violent offenses, which, according to popular notions, form the real crimes, like murder or burglary, are not often committed by women, and even in those cases the public is frequently more inclined to find condoning explanations than if it concerns men. There has always been something pathetic about the disgraced and dishonored woman delinquent in the eyes of the public, whereas male delinquents are usually feared as dangerous criminals who willfully prey upon society, and who therefore generally inspire defensive feelings of hostility and revenge.

Separate reformatories for women did not develop until the late 1800s and were often reluctantly developed by legislatures who were loath to operate a separate institution for such small numbers. After reviewing the development and characteristics of the institutions existing in the late 1920s, Lekkerkerker concluded that, "The most important lesson which may be drawn from the half a century of experience of the American reformatory system so far is that the treatment of women's delinquency is a very different problem from that of male criminality, and that the penal system for women should be considered separately, and not be governed dogmatically by the same principles and methods which are applied to prisons for men."

Although sophisticated, extensive, and insightful, Lekkerker-ker's work received less attention (and remains relatively obscure) compared to a study by Sheldon and Eleanore Glueck a few years later (1934). The Gluecks clearly advanced the multicausal and exhaustively empirical approaches in crimi-nology. Studying almost 500 convicted women, following them up for years after their release, the Gluecks came to the conclusion that mental inferiority, economic hardship, lack of education, and familial instability all played a part in setting the stage for a woman to behave criminally. In fact, so impressed were they with the combination of problems which charac-terized the women they studied that they were compelled to assert:

This swarm of defective, diseased, anti-social misfits, then, comprises the human material which a reformatory and parole system are required by society to transform into wholesome, decent, law-abiding citizens! Is it not a miracle that a proportion of them were actually rehabilitated?

It was the Glueck's unhappy prediction that the "unfortu-nate social heritage" of these criminal women would probably be handed down to a new generation, for a majority of the subjects had children, both legitimate and illegitimate, and almost 80% of the mothers were indifferent if not hostile to their offspring—the "iceberg" theory in operation. During a five year follow-up, most of the women seemed to do a little better, especially while under parole supervision, and so the Gluecks concluded that the institutional and parole programs had "played some part" in improving the offenders in general. But the Gluecks did not credit the reformatory or parole system for very much of the improvement. Rather, they asserted that reform is contingent on the "disposition" of the offender to reform, treatment to which she can be responsive, and chance experiences after release.

Having established that the approach to crime causation ought properly to be multicausal, criminological researchers began inspecting more closely various aspects or factors of female criminality, and thus, during the 1940s, the study of women's criminality entered its fourth stage, which might be called the *numbers and offenses* stage. More and more small-scale studies were devoted to reporting and analyzing the types of crimes committed by women, as well as to attempts to explain why significantly fewer women were criminally adjudicated. These concerns were probably provoked in part by rising rates of female criminality, and in part by increasing rejection of the notion that differences in male and female criminality were due to male superiority; Lombroso's notion of a monstrous "born criminal" type was no longer satisfactory for explaining why the "weaker sex" should be more apt to commit crimes against persons than against property. Researchers became interested in trying to explain certain variations between the patterns of female and male criminality, such as age of peak criminality, types of crimes, and so on. Thus, for example, Cassity in 1941 asserted that age of peak criminality was related to psychological developments. Whereas "male incidence of felony reaches its peak between the ages of 16 and 25," female criminality was found to peak much later, from ages 26 to 30. Cassity's explanation was that "Woman is in her full bloom of attractiveness in the early 20's and as a consequence during those years, she is least beset by the emotional frustrations which she begins to experience after 25."

Cassity also maintained that, while fewer in number, cases of female criminality had deeper psychological meaning than did those of men.

The numbers and types stage ultimately culminated in 1950 with the publication of *The Criminality of Women* by Pollak, one of the most significant works on female criminality to date. Pollak asserted that the difference in numbers of males and females involved in criminal behavior was not as great as official statistics would seem to indicate. The disparity, Pollak maintained, may be attributed to the "masked" quality of women's crimes, which is a function of women's roles in society, the psychological components of femaleness, and certain physical factors. Pollak asserted that the many misconceptions concerning female criminality were due in part to man's sheer inability to understand woman and in part to man's self-deception regarding woman because of an unwillingness to grant her equality. As the oppressor in a male dominated world, man has simultaneously needed and feared woman; thus, he has either idealized her "into a sweetness and purity" which has made her appear harmless, even dependent, or he has condemned her completely. Consequently, "It has been the traditional opinion of criminologists that women commit relatively fewer crimes and that when they do so they somehow betray their womanhood by venturing out into a reserve of men."

Pollak's contribution apparently provoked a new and special attention to female offenders, for the 1950s began to see an increase in special lectures and workshops on female criminality at conferences with nationwide attendance. Also, some of the major correctional periodicals devoted entire issues to a special focus on female criminality. The social role and social status of female offenders began to be taken into consideration in attempts to analyze the differences between male and female crime, and those analyzing the female crime rate kept an eye on the degree of emancipation of women in society.

It was inevitable that new insight into the relationship between woman's social position and her criminality should lead researchers in the 1960s to question the social system of females in reformatories and prisons. The progression to this study marks the entry into the fifth stage of the study of female criminality, which we shall call the *women's prisons stage*. Except for Lekkerkerker's expansive study in the late 1920s, no specific research attention had been paid to the prisons in which women were confined in all the years of their existence. The only literature on the subject up to the 1960s was reports, usually written by wardens, social workers, or other institutional staff, on various aspects of prison programs. Oftentimes these reports were intended to persuade state officials to provide separate institutions for women instead of containing them in a wing or annex of a men's institution, and these reports emphasized the peculiar needs of female prisoners. Other reports were intended primarily for boasting about the achievements or progressive programs of existing women's institutions. And indeed, women's prisons had in many ways been more progressive and innovative than had those for men from the very beginning. They were the first institutions to be operated on the "open" system (no high surrounding walls, perhaps even no fence, and greater interaction with outside community); they were first to develop real classification methods and treatment programs which were individually oriented; they were among the first to reduce idleness to a minimum through extensive work and training programs; they sought to provide not only basic academic and vocational education, but "social education" as well; they were first to operate so called "day parole;" they had from the beginning much more informal visiting arrangements; they were often built upon a "cottage" plan, involving a more homelike atmosphere than would be possible in the penitentiary structure; and they were the first to try "student government" systems, although it is questionable as to how much say inmates actually had under these programs (American Prison Association, 1954). Lekkerkerker (1931) felt that this progressiveness was due to the fact that women were usually appointed to head these institutions and that politics had had little influence over the management, "partly because of improved systems of public control and of appointing the personnel which were adopted for these newer institutions, partly, perhaps, because political activity and competition for jobs is not so keen among women as among men." Also, Lekkerkerker and others felt that the "natural inclination" of women to go into social service meant that women's institutions could attract more highly competent and creative leadership than could men's, while several writers have observed that repressive measures could be discarded more easily in women's prisons because there is simply "less fear of women who commit crimes than there is of men" (Addition, 1957).

In any case, it was such common scientific belief that women prisoners were in better, more progressive institutions that no research into the internal structure of women's prisons was undertaken until the 1960s. Lekkerkerker's study of the development of American reformatories was complemented in 1962 by Smith's study of the treatment of female prisoners in the United Kingdom, in which she asserted that certain treatment programs were more successful and/or appropriate for women than for men in prison and that the needs of females differed from those of men. But Clemmer's *The Prison Community* (1940) and Sykes' *The Society of Captives* (1958) were not matched by comparable studies of American women's institutions until the publication of Ward and Kassebaum's *Women's Prison: Sex and Social Structure* in 1965 and Giallombardo's *Society of Women* in 1966. In fact, up to this point, it seems that criminologists and correctional officials assumed that the inner social structure of women's prisons was virtually similar to that revealed by Clemmer, Sykes, and others in male institutions. Ward and Kassebaum's study and that of Giallombardo are quite similar in that both studies were undertaken to uncover the inner social structure and both focused on homosexual relationships as the basis of that structure and as the prevalent response to the pains experienced by women during incarceration. Ward and Kassebaum found that segregation from family was the most severe deprivation for women in prison, while Giallombardo observed that lack of heterosexual relations was a particular hardship, but voluntary homosexual relations served to soothe both of those deprivations. Clearly, these similar findings point to a vast difference between the social structure in women's prisons and that in male prisons, where homosexuality is generally a brutalizing factor.

CONCLUSION

Since the appearance of these two books in the mid-sixties there have been few other major contributions to the field. There *has* been a general acceleration in the rate at which articles dealing with aspects of female criminality have appeared in professional journals. And, thankfully, there has been a growing sophistication and seriousness about the manner in which the popular media have presented the subject to the public. It is unclear what general direction these most recent additions are taking; we cannot yet pinpoint a distinct sixth stage of research.

We can, however, pinpoint areas of research which clearly *ought* to be focused upon in the years to come if our understanding of female offenders is to be scientifically valid. Certainly the primary, albeit global, assignment is to validate previous criminological findings derived from male samples against female populations. For example, Irwin's 1970 study of the various moral careers of male offenders before, during , and after incarceration may or may not apply to females. Similarly, Glaser's research (1964) on factors associated with recidivism among men has never been validated for women. If the prison social structure studies are any indication, there may be many surprises awaiting us in testing these findings. If present statistical trends continue, there will be more women in prisons and jails than ever before. What are we going to do with them? Will new facilities and programs initiated to accommodate them be blindly modeled after those for males? Certainly, logic dictates that programs for women need to be based on findings *tested* as valid for women, not presumed to be so.

The era in which we live is one in which the statuses and roles of women in society are dramatically changing. The female offender is changing, too. We can no longer rely on criminological knowledge which is untested for validity, incomplete in many areas, and increasingly obsolete.

REFERENCES

ADDITION, H. (1957) "Institutional treatment of women offenders." NPPA J. 3, 1 (January): 21-30.

American Prison Association (1954) A Manual of Correctional Standards. New York.

BISHOP, C. (1931) Women and Crime. London: Chatto & Windus.

BLOS, P. (1969) "Three typical constellations in female delinquency," pp. 99-110 in O. Pollak and A. S. Friedman (eds.) Family Dynamics and Female Sexual Delinquency. Palo Alto, Ca.: Science & Behavior Books.

BURKHART, K. (1971) "Women in prison." Ramparts Magazine 9, 11 (June): 21-29.

CASSITY, J. H. (1941-1942) "Socio-psychiatric aspects of female felons." J. of Criminal Psychopathology 3: 597-604.

CLEMMER, D. (1940) The Prison Community. Boston: Christopher.

FERNALD, M. R., M.H.S. HAYES, and A. DAWLEY (1920) A Study of Women Delinquents in New York State. New York: Century.

GIALLOMBARDO, R. (1966) Society of Women. New York: John Wiley.

GLASER, D. (1964) The Effectiveness of a Prison and Parole System. Indianapolis: Bobbs-Merrill.

GLUECK, S. and E. T. GLUECK (1934) Five Hundred Delinquent Women. New York: Alfred A. Knopf.

IRWIN, J. (1970) The Felon. Englewood Cliffs, N. J. Prentice-Hall.

KRONHAUSEN, P. and E. KRONHAUSEN (1969) Erotic Fantasies: A Study of the Sexual Imagination. New York: Grove Press.

LEKKERKERKER, E. C. (1931) Reformatories for Women in the United States. Holland: J. B. Wolters.

LOMBROSO, C. and W. FERRERO (1958) The Female Offender. New York: Philosophical Library.

POLLAK, O. (1950) The Criminality of Women. Philadelphia: Univ. of Pennsylvania Press.

REEVES, M. (1929) Training Schools for Delinquent Girls.

SMITH, A. D. (1965) "Penal policy and the woman offender," pp. 111-132 in The Sociological Review, Monograph 9. Sociological Studies in the British Penal Services, University of Keele Press (June).

--- (1962) Women in Prison. London: Stevens.

SPAULDING, E. R. (1923) An Experimental Study of Psychopathic Delinquent Women. New York: Rand McNally.

SYKES, G. (1958) The Society of Captives. New Jersey: Princeton Univ. Press.

Uniform Crime Reports (1973) "Crime in the United States: 1972." Washington, D.C.: Government Printing Office.

WARD, D. A. and G. G. KASSEBAUM (1965) Women's Prison: Sex and Social Structure. Chicago: Aldine.

WEIDENSALL, J. (1916) The Mentality of the Criminal Woman. Baltimore: Warwick & York.

PHYSICAL ATTRACTIVENESS OF FEMALE OFFENDERS
Effects on Institutional Performance

HELENE ENID CAVIOR
Robert F. Kennedy Youth Center
Federal Bureau of Prisons
STEVEN C. HAYES and NORMAN CAVIOR
West Virginia University

Physical attractiveness ratings and five measures of institution performance were obtained for 75 female former residents at a federal youth center. Physical attractiveness was found to be significantly related to the number of town trips and the number of high stigma aggressive and high stigma nonaggressive negative behavior reports. In general, the relationships between the other performance measures and physical attractiveness were in the predicted direction. Some relationships between performance measures and physical attractiveness were affected by race of the resident. Results were discussed in terms of other reported findings on the effects of physical attractiveness.

Several recent investigations have indicated that the physical attractiveness of a person plays a significant role in the environmental consequences that the person experiences, both in judicial and nonjudicial settings.

Authors' Note: *This study was conducted with the cooperation of the staff of the Robert F. Kennedy Youth Center, Federal Bureau of Prisons, U.S. Department of Justice. The center is not responsible for the contents of this report; the report does not necessarily represent the center's views. Requests for reprints should be sent to Ms. Helene E. Cavior, Research Department, Robert F. Kennedy Youth Center, Morgantown, West Virginia 26505. The authors would like to thank Ms. Vicki Goodykoontz for her assistance in collecting the data.*

In nonjudicial settings physical attractiveness has been found to be positively correlated with (a) popularity among children (Cavior and Dokecki, 1970; Staffieri, 1967); (b) popularity and dating preferences among adolescents (Berscheid et al., 1971; Byrne et al., 1970; Cavior and Dokecki, 1973); (c) acceptance into college sororities and fraternities (Roff and Brody, 1953); (d) actual dating partners (Murstein, 1972); (e) actual marriage partners (Cavior and Boblett, 1972); and (f) being helped when in a distressful situation (Athanasiou and Greene, 1973), among others.

In judicial settings physical attractiveness has been found to be associated with a number of dependent variables. Three simulated courtroom trial studies have been reported which relate levels of attractiveness to juridic outcomes (Kulka and Kressler, 1973; Shaw, 1972; Sigal and Ostrove, 1973).

Two studies have been reported regarding the importance of physical attractiveness in correctional settings. Cavior and Howard (1973) found that facial pictures of black and white incarcerated male delinquents were judged, by same race raters, significantly less attractive than pictures of corresponding groups of high school students. In addition, significant differences were found among these white delinquents, but not among the black, for Quay's (Quay and Parsons, 1971) four behavioral categories of delinquency.

In a three year field research project, Kurtzberg et al. (1968) found that cosmetic and reconstructive plastic surgery significantly reduced the recidivism rate among adult, nonaddict, male offenders with facial deformities as compared with a control group of offenders with similar facial problems who did not receive surgery. These two studies suggest that low physical attractiveness contributes to careers of deviancy.

Finally, two studies have been reported which examined the effects of physical attractiveness in psychotherapeutic settings. Cavior and Glowgower (1973) found that the interaction between the physical attractiveness of male therapists and the physical attractiveness of their female clients had a significant effect on the number of individual psychotherapy sessions.

Choban et al. (1974) found that the physical attractiveness of chronic hospitalized, female "mental" patients was more positively correlated with discharge from the hospital than was the number of tokens earned by the patients, and that physical attractiveness was positively correlated with the number of tokens earned. These two studies suggest that what happens to females, as well as males, in treatment settings, is in part a function of their level of physical attractiveness.

This brings us to the purpose of the present investigation. No studies have been reported which examine the effects of the degree of attractiveness of female offenders on program performance in correctional settings. Based on the review of the literature and the constraints of the data available, five hypotheses were tested in the present study: attractive female offenders, as compared with less attractive offenders, would have (a) fewer offenses involving aggression, (b) fewer negative behavior reports, (c) more positive notations, (d) more town trips, and (e) more preferable outcomes (parole versus mandatory release versus escape).

METHOD

SUBJECTS AND SETTING

The subjects were 75 female, former students (inmates) at the Robert F. Kennedy Youth Center, a coed minimum security federal prison. The sample was composed of all of the women who resided in one of the two female cottages who were discharged from the Kennedy Youth Center prior to March 15, 1974. Twelve of the original 87 subjects were dropped from the sample because of incomplete data. Students from only one cottage were included because the two cottages operate very different treatment programs and some of the dependent measures have different meanings in the two cottages. The cottage with the larger sample was used in this study.

The students ranged in age from 15 to 26 years, with a mean age of 19.4 years. Forty-four subjects were black and 31 were white. Their length of stay at the Kennedy Youth Center ranged from 11 to 577 days with a mean of 301 days.

PHYSICAL ATTRACTIVENESS RATINGS

A front facial picture was obtained from each student's file and coded on the back. Raters looked at all the pictures first and then sorted each picture into one of seven physical attractiveness categories from (1) very unattractive to (7) very attractive. The deck of pictures was shuffled before each rater sorted them. The pictures of blacks and whites were mixed together and raters were told that the purpose of the study was to examine the effects of the physical attractiveness of the women on a number of variables and not to make comparisons between their physical attractiveness ratings of black and white subjects. The final score for each student was determined by a mean of raters' scores.

Ten white, male raters from West Virginia University judged the pictures. The raters ranged in age from 18 to 35 years, with a mean age of 24.8 years. White, male raters were used because the great majority of persons working in the correctional area are white males. In addition, previous research has shown that male and female ratings of physical attractiveness are highly correlated (Cavior and Dokecki, 1973; Cavior and Howard, 1973) as are those between white and black raters (Cavior and Howard, 1973).

DEPENDENT MEASURES

To collect data on the students' precipitating offense and in-program performance, their institutional files were examined and the following variables extracted:

(a) Offense type. Precipitating offenses which resulted in the present commitment were divided into aggressive and nonaggressive types, coded 1 and 2 respectively, for statistical analysis. A more specific division was not possible due to the contaminating effects of plea bargaining and the small sample sizes that would have resulted.

(b) Negative behavior reports. The Kennedy Youth Center uses a notation system for recording all nonserious negative behaviors and an incident report system for recording serious negative behaviors. For the purposes of this study negative notations and incident reports were combined. A categorization for offense types developed by Chan (1974) was modified so that it was applicable for classifying the negative behavior reports: (1) aggression based—destructive violence, e.g., fighting with or without weapons; (2) aggression based—harmful malice, e.g., use of weapons to threaten or intimidate; (3) nonaggression based—high stigma, e.g., possession of large quantities of illegal drugs or alcohol, interfering with the institution count, extreme disrespect toward staff; and (4) nonaggression based—mild sanction, e.g., violation of institution rules such as being late for or absent from class or chore and wearing unauthorized clothing. All negative behavior reports were divided into these four categories and further divided into whether the behavior occurred during the first three months at the Kennedy Youth Center, or after that. These divisions were made in part to enable a comparison between offense type and negative behavior type across time. To test the effect of physical attractiveness, the four negative behavior categories were collapsed across time.

(c) Positive notations. These are similar to the negative notations except noting positive behavior. The total number received by each student was compiled.

(d) Town trips. The Kennedy Youth Center operates a program whereby students may go to town occasionally. There are two types: escorted and unescorted. Escorted town trips may be taken by students of lower program status and are easier to obtain, providing the student can secure an approved escort. Unescorted town trips are more difficult to obtain, and are essentially unsupervised. Both types of town trips can only be taken by students in good standing in the program and are subject to well-defined approval procedures. The total number of both types of town trips was obtained for each student.

(e) Outcome. The in-program outcome was divided into three types: (1) escape or disciplinary transfer, (2) expiration or mandatory release, and (3) parole either directly to the community or via transfer to a community treatment center. The three types of outcomes were coded 1, 2, and 3 respectively, for statistical analysis, since they represent a successful outcome continuum.

RESULTS

To facilitate the comparison of different student's performance, negative behavior reports, positive notations, and town trips were changed into rate measures by dividing them by the number of days served at the Kennedy Youth Center.

Physical attractiveness scores were divided into attractive (equal to or greater than 4.0) and unattractive (less than 4.0). The hypotheses regarding the dependent measures were tested with a 2 x 2 factorial analysis of variance using a least squares technique with race and physical attractiveness as the independent variables.

Race was used as an independent variable because it was suspected that physical attractiveness would operate differently for blacks and whites (Cavior and Howard, 1973). The physical attractiveness ratings of blacks ranged from 1.8 to 5.2 with a mean of 3.35. Thirty-four black students were in the low physical attractiveness group and ten were in the high group. Ratings of white students ranged from 1.2 to 6.1 with a mean of 4.04. Fourteen white students were in the low physical attractiveness group and 17 were in the high group.

A chi-square test of independence indicated that race and physical attractiveness were not independent ($X^2 = 8.14$, $p < .01$). The correlation between these two variables was .33 ($p < .01$).

All of the F tests have 1/71 degrees of freedom. Physical attractiveness main effects which tested the five hypotheses were evaluated using one-tailed F tests, while race main effects and interactions were evaluated using two-tailed F tests. A correlation matrix was also generated.

The results did not support hypothesis a: physical attractiveness had no apparent effect on the offense for which subjects were committed. Inspection of the data indicated that only five of the 75 subjects had been committed for aggressive offenses. However, of the five who were committed for aggressive offenses, four were in the low physical attractiveness category.

The data partially supported hypothesis b. For the nonaggressive—high stigma category a significant main effect for physical attractiveness (F = 3.17, p < .05) was found, indicating that low attractive offenders engage in more of this type of behavior than high attractive offenders. A similar finding was obtained for the actual aggressive category (F = 2.76, p < .05). For the other two negative behavior categories (aggression to intimidate and nonaggression—low stigma) low physical attractiveness offenders engaged in more of these negative behaviors than the high physical attractiveness offenders, although the differences were not statistically significant. There were no main effects due to race, nor any significant interactions, although there was a tendency for the blacks to receive slightly more negative notations than whites.

Hypothesis c was not supported. There was a significant negative correlation for blacks between physical attractiveness and positive notations (r = −.31, p < .05, two-tailed test), which is an opposite effect from that predicted. The correlation between physical attractiveness and positive notations for whites was positive but did not approach statistical significance. The analysis of variance revealed a trend toward an interaction effect (F = 1.96, p < .16).

The analysis of variance of total town trips yielded significant effects for race (F = 5.04, p .< .03), physical attractiveness (F = 4.31, p < .05) and the race by physical attractiveness interaction (F = 3.62, p < .06), thus supporting hypothesis d. The interaction was due to the strong effect of physical attractiveness on town trips received by white students and the lack of effect of physical attractiveness on town trips received by black students. In correlational terms, physical attractiveness correlated .40 (p < .01) with town trips for whites and −.09 (p < .55) for blacks. When broken down into escorted and unescorted town trips, physical attractiveness was found to have similar effects on the two types of town trips.

The data failed to support hypothesis e; that is, no significant effects of physical attractiveness were found on the type of outcome (parole, expiration, escape, or disciplinary transfer). However, the same trend was found as was predicted, namely, high physical attractiveness subjects tended to receive more paroles and expirations than low physical attractiveness subjects.

One of the implications of a behavioral trait model (consistency of behavior across situations) for corrections is that persons committed for aggressive offenses should exhibit more aggressive behavior while incarcerated than persons committed for nonaggressive offenses, at least during the first few months before a treatment program is likely to have much effect. Although not related to the central notion of this study, the data did enable an evaluation of the above hypothesis. No significant correlation was found between offense type and type of negative reports received. It was found, however, that there was a large correlation between the number of negative behavior reports in the first three months at the Kennedy Youth Center and those after that time ($r = .66$, $p < .0001$). This indicates a high degree of consistency of response to the Kennedy Youth Center environment.

DISCUSSION

The Kennedy Youth Center is a highly structured institution emphasizing the use of criteria and goals in determining the progress of a student. Nevertheless, it is clear that physical attractiveness affected a number of measures which may have an important impact on the incarcerated female.

The present study found that while at the Kennedy Youth Center female offenders of below average attractiveness, as compared with those of above average attractiveness, were committed for more aggressive offenses, engaged in more nonaggressive—high stigma behaviors, and received fewer town trips. Although the following differences were not statistically significant, below average attractive offenders obtained less successful outcomes than the above average attractive females and were incarcerated for more aggressive crimes.

There is an unexplained race effect present in the relationship between physical attractiveness and positive notations. For blacks, it was the only variable for which the results were opposite from the predicted direction. It is possible that positive notations tended to be given primarily to students who had previously gotten into trouble. That is, if a student arrives at the institution and gets into trouble, more attention is likely to be given to any positive behaviors on her part, resulting in more positive notations. However, whites who receive more negative behavior reports tend to receive fewer positive notations. This may have something to do with differential staff expectations of the behavior of the two races.

It is suspected that part of the effect of race was due to the fact that only facial pictures were used. It is likely that more racial differences are apparent in the face (e.g., lips, noses, hair) than in the rest of the body. It is also likely that not only would racial effects have been reduced but that physical attractiveness would have had a greater effect if full length pictures (and more preferably, the subjects themselves) had been available for ratings of physical attractiveness. The interaction of race effects and physical attractiveness effects needs a good deal more research in a variety of settings before its psychological significance can be fully understood.

The physical attractiveness ratings were found to be distributed somewhat differently for each of the races, with whites obtaining higher ratings than blacks. The 2 x 2 (race by physical attractiveness group) chi-square indicated that the two factors were not totally independent. In a natural environment it is probably impossible to find physical attractiveness and race completely independent of each other. For example, lightness of skin color was preferred to darkness among whites in Texas (Cavior, 1970), among Mexicans in Mexico (Cavior and Dokecki, 1970), and among blacks in Georgia (Cavior and Howard, 1973).

The tendency for institutional outcomes to be affected by physical attractiveness may be mediated by the even stronger effects of physical attractiveness on negative behavior. That is, low attractive offenders receive more negative behavior reports and it is these negative behavior reports which result in less desirable outcomes.

As of yet, the exact mechanism of the effects of physical attractiveness has not been determined. It seems likely that the differing environmental consequences for attractive versus unattractive individuals may shape divergent behavioral repertoires. The relationship between aggression-based behavior and physical attractiveness is perhaps one such example. If attractive individuals are reacted to more positively they may find less reason for recourse to violent means to achieve their goals. Conversely, unattractive individuals may experience more frustration due to their relative lack of access to important reinforcing events, thus increasing the likelihood of aggression.

The findings of the present study are congruent with the previous literature regarding the effects of physical attractiveness on behavior. However, it appears that the magnitude of the effects of physical attractiveness are small in therapeutic settings which utilize specific criteria and goals for behavior change. Physical attractiveness had a smaller effect in the study with mental patients (Choban et al., 1974) and in the present study, both of which were conducted at institutions which employ token economies, than in the one-to-one traditional type of therapeutic setting (Cavior and Glowgower, 1973). Consequently, it would appear that it is possible to minimize the effects of physical attractiveness and that steps can be taken to avoid penalizing those female offenders with a relative lack of physical attractiveness.

REFERENCES

ATHANASIOU, R. and P. GREENE (1973) "Physical attractiveness and helping behavior." Proceedings of the Eighty-First Annual Convention of the American Psychological Association 8: 289-290.

BERSCHEID, E., K. DION, E. WALSTER, and G. M. WALSTER (1971) "Physical attractiveness and dating choice: a test of the matching hypothesis." J. of Experimental Social Psychology 7: 173-189.

BYRNE, D., C. R. ERVIN, and J. C. LAMBERTH (1970) "Continuity between the experimental study of attraction and real life computer dating." J. of Personality and Social Psychology 16: 157-165.

CAVIOR, N. (1970) "Physical attractiveness, perceived attitude similarity, and interpersonal attraction among fifth and eleventh grade boys and girls." Ph.D. dissertation. University of Houston.

––– and P. J. BOBLETT (1972) "Physical attractiveness of dating versus married couples." Proceedings of the Eightieth Annual Convention of the American Psychological Association 7: 175-176.

CAVIOR, N. and P. R. DOKECKI (1973) "Physical attractiveness, perceived attitude similarity, and academic achievement as contributors to interpersonal attraction among adolescents." Developmental Psychology 9: 44-54.

––– (1970) "Physical attractiveness and interpersonal attraction among fifth grade boys: a replication with Mexican children." Presented at the meeting of the Southwestern Psychological Association, St. Louis, Missouri, April 25.

CAVIOR, N. and F. GLOWGOWER (1973) "Effects of physical attractiveness of therapist and client on number of psychotherapy sessions." Proceedings of the Eighty-First Annual Convention of the American Psychological Association 8: 1069-1970.

CAVIOR, N. and L. R. HOWARD (1973) "Facial attractiveness and juvenile delinquency among black and white offenders." J. of Abnormal Child Psychology 1: 202-213.

CHAN, J. (1974) "A proposed typology of criminal offenses." Unpublished manuscript. West Virginia University.

CHOBAN, M. C., N. CAVIOR, and P. BENNETT (1974) "Effects of physical attractiveness of patients on outcome in a token economy." Unpublished manuscript. West Virginia University.

KULKA, R. A. and J. B. KESSLER (1973) "Is justice really blind?–the influence of physical attractiveness on decisions of simulated jurors." Presented at the Convention of the Speech Communication Association, New York City.

KURTZBERG, R. L., H. SAFAR, and N. CAVIOR (1968) "Surgical and social rehabilitation of adult offenders." Proceedings of the Seventy-Sixth Annual Convention of the American Psychological Association 3: 649-650.

MURSTEIN, B. I. (1972) "Physical attractiveness and marital choice." J. of Personality and Social Psychology 22: 8-12.

QUAY, H. C. and L. B. PARSONS (1971) "The differential behavioral classification of the juvenile offender." Federal Bureau of Prisons, Department of Justice. Washington, D.C.: Government Printing Office.

ROFF, M. and D. S. BRODY (1953) "Appearance and choice status during adolescence." J. of Personality 36: 347-356.

SHAW, J. I. (1972) "Reactions to victims and defendants of varying degrees of attractiveness." Psychonomic Sci. 27: 329-330.

SIGALL, H. and N. OSTROVE (1973) "Effects of the physical attractiveness of the defendant and nature of the crime on juridic judgement." Proceedings of the Eighty-First Annual Convention of the American Psychological Association 8: 177-178.

STAFFIERI, J. R. (1967) "A study of social stereotype of body image in children." J. of Personality and Social Psychology 1: 101-104.

PERSONALITY DIFFERENCES BETWEEN MALE AND FEMALE PRISON INMATES
Measured by the MMPI

JAMES H. PANTON
State of North Carolina
Department of Social Rehabilitation and Control

Most of the research on classification of prisoners has been conducted solely with male samples. The present study compared MMPI profiles of male and female prisoners. Males showed significantly higher means on Hs and D and females on Si and Pa, particularly the Pa2 subscale. Both sexes has elevated Pd scales. It was concluded that male inmates appear to be more anti-social with neurotic overlays, while the female inmates appear more asocial than anti-social with overlays of greater emotional sensitivity—a finding supportive of a continuation of similar adolescent behavioral characteristics of Hathaway and Monachesi.

The female population of the various state and federal prisons presents a significant minority whose needs in terms of proper classification, treatment, and training are as great as the needs of their more numerous male counterparts. Although the majority of prisons provides identical classification for males and females, most of the research in the field of prison classification has been conducted solely with male samples. It would appear that, if research findings are to be effectively utilized in the classification and treatment of both male and female prisoners, both sexes must be employed in research endeavors. One initial goal of such research would seem to be to determine if there are any significant personality differences appearing between male and female prisoners, such differences providing the basis for shaping the treatment and training programs to meet the needs of both sexes. The purpose of this study is to test the hypothesis that there are male-female personality differences appearing within a state prison population, and that these differences can be detected by objective test measurements.

Previous MMPI research with female populations has been somewhat meager and has been primarily in the areas of developing female scale norms (Bavernfield, 1956; Dahlstrom et al., 1972; Weisgerber, 1954), screening for occuptional and educational selection (Beaver, 1953; Black, 1954), studies of student populations, (Beier, 1953; Forsyth, 1967; Mahler, 1955; Zeaman, 1958), and psychiatric diagnosis and treatment (Aaronson, 1958; Eichman, 1961; Pauker, 1966a, 1966b; Webb, 1970). Hathaway and Monachesi (1969) have studied the MMPI patterns of large samples of adolescent delinquents and found that girls display more feelings of inferiority than boys, are more sensitive, more easily hurt and more resentful; whereas the MMPI profiles of the boys demonstrated a greater need to be independent of the controls of their society.

Examination of the case history data on the inmate male and female populations, from which the samples for this study were drawn, reveals that the females were more likely to come from shattered homes, have greater difficulty in their interpersonal relationships with family and peers, and present a greater instance of marital incompatibility. In addition 24% of the females compared to 12% of the males presented records of having been treated for mental problems. The males were more inclined toward the excessive use of alcohol, and presented more extensive prior criminal records.

METHOD

A sample of 128 female admissions to the North Carolina Correctional System who presented valid MMPI protocols (L < 70, F < 85, K < 70) were matched as to age, race, IQ, and education with an equal number of male admissions. Table 1 presents the demographic criteria employed in the selection of

TABLE 1
COMPARISON OF AGE, IQ, AND EDUCATION FOR 128
MALE AND 128 FEMALE PRISON INMATES

	Males (n=128)		Females (n=128)	
	Mean	SD	Mean	SD
Age	29.2	9.4	29.2	9.0
IQ	91.3	10.3	91.2	10.6
Education	8.5	2.2	8.5	2.1

NOTE: Of both male and female subjects, 66.4% were white. The remaining subjects were Negro.

the samples—each of these factors having previously been reported as exercising influence on MMPI scores (Panton, 1959, 1960; Winfield, 1953; Applezweig, 1948). The mean MMPI profiles of the two groups were compared for significant differences appearing between individual MMPI scales. The t-test was employed to test the statistical level of the mean differences. Further subscale analysis was performed on the MMPI regular clinical scale showing the most significant difference appearing between the male and female samples.

RESULTS AND DISCUSSION

Table 2 presents the comparison of the means and standard deviations of the two samples on the regular diagnostic scales of the MMPI. T-ratios are presented for those scales producing mean differences significant at or beyond the .01 level of statistical confidence. The significant elevation of the male means above the female on the Hs and D scales implies that the male inmates are more prone to voice physical complaints, more pessimistic in their outlook on life, and are more inclined toward irritability and emotional immaturity. The greater mean elevation of the females on the Si scale reveals that the females are significantly more deviant than the males. The females appear more inclined toward withdrawal from social intercourse

TABLE 2
**COMPARISON OF MMPI AND STANDARD DEVIATIONS FOR
128 MALE AND 128 FEMALE PRISON INMATES**

Scales	Hs	D	Hy	Pd	Mf	Pa	Pt	Sc	Ma	Si
Males										
Mean	61.2	64.2	58.8	70.4	52.5	58.1	60.4	63.2	60.5	53.7
SD	15.0	10.8	11.0	10.1	9.4	11.6	10.8	14.0	10.8	8.4
Code: 4'28179—365/[a]					Code: 4'28179—365/[a]					
Females										
Mean	55.4	60.4	56.7	70.8	53.3	64.2	57.5	60.1	58.2	58.1
SD	12.2	9.2	11.6	12.1	8.9	13.5	8.4	10.3	10.1	8.4
Code: 4'628—79315/					Code: 4'628—79315/					
M/Diff	5.9	3.9	2.1	.4	.8	6.1	2.9	3.1	2.2	4.4
t-Ratio	3.4[b]	3.1				3.9[b]				4.2[b]

a. Welsh's system of coding.
b. p $<$.01.

and have feelings of being less confident than the males in their ability to cope with socioeconomic demands of society.

The elevation of the mean Pa score for the females considerably above that of the males can be more closely interpreted if the scale is broken down into its subscale components. Three subscales have been established by Harris and Lingoes (1955). They are briefly described as follows:

Pa1: Ideas of external influence which indicates the experiencing of frankly persecutory ideas; externalization of blame for difficulties; frustrations.

Pa2: Thinking of oneself as something special and different from others; thinking of oneself as high-strung; cherishing of sensitive feelings; overly subjective.

Pa3: Affirmation of moral virtue; excessive generosity about voiced obliviousness to other peoples' hostility.

Pa1 expresses paranoid ideation as portrayed in frankly psychotic people; Pa2 is often associated with borderline conditions of a prepsychotic nature; and Pa3 correlates with Hy and is found frequently among hysterical people. The emergence of hostile feelings is traceable from repression (Pa3) to projection (Pa1). Table 3 compares the means and standard deviations of the two samples on the Pa subscales. It appears that the Pa scale difference appearing between the groups as indicated by the data in Table 2 is primarily contributable to differences appearing on the Pa2 subscale. This configuration implies for the females a greater sensitivity of feeling, an overly subjectiveness, and the feeling of being different and not easily understood by others.

Both group profiles are distinguished by an elevated mean Pd score of almost identical magnitude. Pd T-scores of approximately seventy are generally characteristic of the majority of prison group profiles. Although the male and female mean Pd scores appear equal on the surface, an examination of the item responses on the Pd scale for both groups reveals that the males respond in greater frequency to items denoting authority conflict characterized by resentment of social demands and conventions; whereas, the females respond more frequently to items implying feelings of isolation and lack of gratification in social relationships.

The male sample presents a 428 (Pd, D, Sc) profile code (see Table 2), which has been found to be characteristic of male inmate samples with IQs below the normal mean of 100 (Panton, 1960); however, the female code is 4628 (Pd, Pa, D, Sc) which underscores the significance of the Pa (6) ranking in the female mean profile. Pa is second in score magnitude in the female mean profile; whereas, it is ranked only ninth in score magnitude in the mean male profile.

TABLE 3
COMPARISON OF MEAN AND STANDARD DEVIATIONS OF Pa
SUBSCALES FOR 128 MALES AND 128 FEMALE PRISON INMATES

Subscales	Males (n=128)		Females (n=128)		M/Diff	T-ratio
	Mean	SD	Mean	SD		
Pa1	51.9	10.2	52.8	10.7	.9	n.s.
Pa2	50.0	9.6	56.2	10.6	6.2	4.9[a]
Pa3	48.2	9.2	50.5	10.0	2.3	n.s.

a. p < .01.

SUMMARY

The responses of 128 female prison inmates to the regular MMPI diagnostic scales were compared to the responses of a sample of 128 male prison inmates in an attempt to assess any personality differences appearing between the two groups. The groups were matched as to race, age, education, and IQ at the time of selection. Only MMPI protocols with validity scale scores within the normal limits were used in the study (L < 70, F < 85, K < 70).

The mean profile of the females was significantly less deviant than the mean profile for the males on the Hs and D scales, implying for the males a greater trend toward employing defenses characterized by over concern with physical functioning, poor morale, voiced pessimism, emotional immaturity, and irritability. The females were significantly more deviant than the males on the Pa and Si scales which implied an over subjectivity and sensitivity, and a greater inclination to avoid establishing meaningful social relationships. Both groups scored abnormally high on the Pd scale, the males scoring predominantly more frequently on those Pd items associated with overt conflict with authority, and the females scoring more frequently on those items associated with feelings of isolation and lack of personal pleasure derived from social intercourse. There were no significant differences appearing between the group comparisons on the Hy, Mf, Pt, Sc, or Ma scales.

The male inmates appear to present a more anti-social sociopathic mean MMPI profile with overlays of neurotic type materials, which reflects the inmate male population's history of greater alcohol abuse and more extensive prior criminality. In contrast, the female inmate's mean profile appears more asocial than anti-social with overlays of greater emotional sensitivity, which is also a reflection of the inmate female population's history, which demonstrated considerable asocialization and emotional problems of adjustment. The independence of social control for the boys and the greater sensitivity and resentfulness of the girls found by Hathaway and Monachesi (1969) in their adolescent profiles appear to be early manifestations of the same type of behavioral characteristics as demonstrated by the adult inmate profiles employed in this study. Longitudinal studies employing the same population samples would be required to establish the significance of this apparent behavioral trend from adolescent to adulthood.

REFERENCES

AARONSON, B. S. (1958) "Age and sex influence on MMPI profile peak distributions in an abnormal population." J. Consulting Psychology 22: 203-206.

APPLEZWEIG, M. H. (1948) "A statistical analysis of the influence of age, education, and intelligence on the scales of the Minnesota Multiphasic Personality Inventory." J. of the Colorado-Wyoming Academy of Sci. 3, 59. (abstract)

BAVERNFIELD, R. H. (1956) "Are sex norms necessary?" J. Counseling Psychology 3: 57-63.

BEAVER, A. (1953) "Personality factors in choice of nursing." J. of Applied Psychology 37: 374-379.

BEIER, E. G. (1953) "The parental identification of male and female college students." J. Abnormal Social Psychology 48: 569-572.

BLACK, J. D. (1954) "A study of the efficiency of the MMPI for screening college women." Amer. Psychologist 9.

DAHLSTROM, W. G., G. S. WELSH, and L. E. DAHLSTROM (1972) "T-score conversion for Harris-Lingoes subscales—female tables," in W. G. Dahlstrom and G. S. Welsh (eds.) MMPI Handbook, Volume 1, Clinical Interpretation. Minneapolis: Univ. of Minnesota Press.

EICHMAN, W. J. (1961) "Replicated factors on the MMPI with female N. P. patients." J. Consulting Psychology 25: 55-60.

FORSYTH, R. P. (1967) "MMPI related behavior in a student nurse group." J. Clinical Psychology 23: 224-229.

HARRIS, R. E. and J. C. LINGOES (1955) "Subscales for the MMPI: an aid to profile interpretation." University of California Department of Psychiatry. (mimeo)

HATHAWAY, S. R. and E. D. MONACHESI (1969) Adolescent Personality and Behavior. Minneapolis: Univ. of Minnesota Press.

MAHLER, I. (1955) "Use of the MMPI with student nurses." J. Applied Psychology 39: 190-193.

PANTON, J. H. (1960) "MMPI code configuration as related to measures of intelligence among a state prison population." J. Social Psychology 51: 403-407.

——— (1959) "Inmate personality differences related to recidivism, age, and race as measured by the MMPI." J. of Correctional Psychology 4: 28-35.

PAUKER, J. D. (1966a) "Stability of MMPI profiles of female psychiatric inpatients." J. Clinical Psychology 22: 209-212.

——— (1966b) "Identification of MMPI profile types in a female, inpatient, psychiatric setting using the Marks and Seeman rules." J. Consulting Psychology 30.

WEBB, J. T. (1970) "Regional and sex differences in MMPI scale high-point frequencies of psychiatric patients." Amer. Psychologist 25.

WEISGERBER, C. A. (1954) "Norms for the MMPI with student nurses." J. of Clinical Psychology 10: 192-194.

WINFIELD, D. (1953) "The relationship between IQ scores and Minnesota Multiphasic Personality Inventory scores." J. of Social Psychology 38.

ZEAMAN, J. B. (1958) "Some of the personality attributes related to achievement in college: a comparison of men and women students." Dissertation Abstracts 18.

THE ADULT FEMALE OFFENDER
A Selected Bibliography

FRANCYNE GOYER-MICHAUD
School of Criminology
Université de Montréal

This bibliography includes more than 200 articles in French or English that have appeared in specialized journals published in at least one of these two languages, from 1959 to 1974 inclusive. It concerns the various problems relating to delinquency or crime among young adult and adult females. The articles are classified in alphabetical order according to author and each title is accompanied by a code letter referring to the relevant heading (or headings) under which it falls.

It is perhaps a little pretentious to call the present work a bibliography as it is not as fully exhaustive as the term implies. Rather, this is a selective bibliography dealing with the following areas:

(1) It pertains to problems that concern only adult women, 18 years of age and older (which is the typical age of the criminal majority).

(2) It bears on the different aspects connected with women who have been judged either delinquents, or in a state of physical or moral danger (before the age of 18 but still in the correctional network), or criminals. The problems of deviance and maladjustment which do not fall under the provisions of a criminal sanction, e.g.,

Author's Note: *I wish to thank Lise Brunet-Aubry for her invaluable assistance and collaboration.*

alcoholism, have been eliminated unless the women concerned have already been legally labelled. In order not to unnecessarily overload this study, a number of articles, particularly those on abortion and attempted suicide, were not included unless they concerned women who had appeared in court on these or other charges.

(3) It includes only articles in English or French that have appeared in specialized professional journals during the period 1959 through 1974. Books, dissertations, and conference proceedings were not cited.

Despite these limitations, this bibliography is intended as an instrument that will afford a broader view of criminality among women and serve to provide material for practitioner and researcher alike.

To attain this goal, the 221 selected articles are classified in alphabetical order according to author, and each title is followed by a code letter referring to the relevant heading (or headings) under which it falls. The significance of the code letter is as follows.

At: Attitudes and values.

Ca: Case report—including case study or case history, and illustrative case.

Co: Comparative study. Under this heading are to be found all comparisons according to age, sex, ethnic origin, type of crime, legal, civil, socioeconomic status, and so on.

Fo: Follow-up, longitudinal, and predictive study.

In: Institutions—their description and functioning.

Mi: Miscellaneous—included here are all titles insufficient in number to be placed under special headings, such as forensic medicine, victimology, biography, and the like. It should be noted that an article may appear under this heading only, or under another as well.

Pe: Personality. In order to avoid overlapping, this includes all the various descriptive and etiological aspects of the offender's personality: criminological, psychiatric, psychological, sociological, sociopsychological.

Se: Sentencing.

So: Somatic aspects—including illnesses, medical care, medicines, physical attributes, physiology.

St: Statistics, type of offence, or inappropriate behaviour. In order not to make the bibliography unwieldy, these headings were grouped together.

Th: Theoretical and general observations—on one or another aspect of female criminality, including legislation.

Tr: Treatment—all forms of treatment as well as behaviour during treatment.

Ty: Typology—of offenders.

AHUJA, R. (1970) "Female murderers in India: a sociological study." Indian J. of Social Work 31: 271-284. [Mi Pe St Ty]
ANDERSON, C. M. (1967) "The female criminal offender." Amer. J. of Correction 29, 6: 7-9. [Th]
ARAI, N. and M. KATO (1970) "Female shoplifting and depressive states." Acta criminologiae et medicinae legalis japonica 36: 28-29. [Ca Pe So St]
ARROWSMITH, P. (1961) "My crime." Twentieth Century 170 (Autumn): 111-117. [Mi]
BADONNEL, M. (1966) "Vol et comportement névrotique" ("Theft and neurotic behaviour"). Revue pénitentiaire et de droit pénal 90: 815-819. [Pe St]
BAILEY, K. G. (1970) "Audiotape self-confrontation in group psychotherapy." Psychological Reports 27: 439-444. [Co Tr]
BEDFORD, A. (1974) "Women and parole." British J. of Criminology 14: 106-117. [Fo St Tr]

BERTHELOT, M. (1968) "Vols commis par les femmes dans les grands magasins" ("Thefts committed by women in large stores"). International Police Chronicle 16, 89: 33-47. [Ca St]

BERTRAND, M. A. (1969) "Self-image and delinquency: a contribution to the study of female criminality and woman's image." Acta criminologica 2: 71-144. [Co Pe]

BILEK, A. J. and A. S. GANZ (1965) "The B-girl problem—a proposed ordinance." J. of Criminal Law, Criminology, and Police Sci. 56: 39-44. [Th]

BLUESTONE, H., E. P. O'MALLEY, and S. CONNEL (1966) "Homosexuals in prison." Corrective Psychiatry and J. of Social Therapy 12: 13-24. [Ca St Tr]

BRICK, H., W. H. DOUB Jr., and W. C. PERDUE (1965) "A comparison of the effects of amitriptyline and protriptyline on anxiety and depressive states in female prisoners." International J. of Neuropsychiatry 1: 325-336. [Pe So]

BROSKOWSKI, A., R. SILVERMANN, and H. HINKEL (1971) "Actuarial assessment of criminality in women." Criminology 9: 166-184. [Co Pe]

BROWN, F. and P. EPPS, (1966). "Childhood bereavement and subsequent crime ." British Journal of Psychiatry 112: 1043-1048. [Co Pe]

BRUMMIT, H. (1963) "Observations on drug addicts in a house of detention for women." Corrective Psychiatry and J. of Social Therapy 9: 62-70. [Pe St Tr]

BRYAN, J. H. (1965) "Apprenticeships in prostitution." Social Problems 12: 287-297. [St]

BUCOVE, A. D. (1968) "A case of prepartum psychosis and infanticide." Psychiatric Q. 42: 263-270. [Ca Pe St]

BURKE, J. L. (1963) "A study of female offenders under psychiatric observation." Corrective Psychiatry and J. of Social Therapy 9: 78-85. [Co In Pe]

BUWALDA, M. (1963) "California institution for women." Correctional Rev. (September-October): 13-15. (International bibliography on crime and delinquency, 1965, 2: 10380) [In]

Canadian Corrections Association (1969) "Brief on the woman offender." Canadian J. of Corrections 11: 26-60. [Co In Se St Th Tr]

CARPENTER, S. R. (1966) "An experiment in successful living." California Youth Authority Q. 19, 4: 9-14. [Tr]

CASSEL, R. N. and J. CLAYTON (1961) "A preliminary analysis of certain social self-concepts of women in a correctional institution." Sociology and Social Research 45: 316-319. [Pe]

CHAUDHURY, S. C. (1973) "Some thoughts on immoral traffic in women in Calcutta." Social Defence 8, 32: 13-18. [St Th]

CHWAST, J. (1971) "Special problems in treating female offenders: sociopsychological aspects." International J. of Offender Therapy 15: 24-27. [Pe Tr]

CLONINGER, C. R. and S. B. GUZE (1973a) "Psychiatric disorders and criminal recidivism: a follow-up study of female criminals." Archives of General Psychiatry 29: 266-269. [Fo Pe]

——— (1973b) "Psychiatric illnesses in the families of female criminals: a study of 288 first-degree relatives." British J. of Psychiatry 122: 697-703. [Mi]

——— (1970) "Psychiatric illness and female criminality: the role of sociopathy and hysteria in the anti-social woman." Amer. J. of Psychiatry 127: 303-311. [Pe]

COCHRANE, R. (1971) "The structure of value systems in male and female prisoners." British J. of Criminology 11: 73-79. [At Co]

COLE, K. E., G. FISHER, and S. S. COLE (1968) "Women who kill: a sociopsychological study." Archives of General Psychiatry 19: 1-8. [Ca Pe St Ty]

COLEMAN, B. I. (1974) "Helping women addicts in New York City." International J. of Offender Therapy and Comp. Criminology 18: 82-85. [Ca St Tr]

Committee on Public Health of the New York Academy of Medicine (1965) "Medical examination in the women's house of detention." Bull. of the New York Academy of Medicine 41: 1104. [So]

CRAMER, M. J. and E. BLACKER (1963) " 'Early' and 'late' problem drinkers among female prisoners." J. of Health and Human Behaviour 4: 282-290. [Co Pe St]

CUNNINGHAM, G. (1963) "Supervision of the female offender." Federal Probation 27, 4: 12-16.[Tr]

DALTON, K. (1961) "Menstruation and crime." British Medical J. 2: 1752-1753. [So]

DAS, M. N. (1960) "Female infanticide among the Khonds of Orissa." Man in India 40: 30-35. [Mi St]

DEADMAN, W. J. (1964) "Infanticide." Canadian Medical Assn. J. 91: 558-560. [Ca Mi St]

DELL, S. and T.C.N. GIBBENS (1971) "Remands of women offenders for medical reports." Medicine, Sci. and the Law 11: 117-127. [Co Pe]

DEMONE, H. W., Jr. (1963) "Experiments in referral to alcoholism clinics." Q. J. of Studies on Alcohol 24: 495-502. [St Tr]

DENNETT, R. and J. S. YORK (1966) "Group therapy in one women's correctional institution." Amer. J. of Correction 28, 1: 21-25. [Tr]

DENYS, R. G. (1969) "Lady paperhangers." Canadian J. of Corrections 11: 165-192. [Pe St]

DESHAIES, G. (1962) "L'alcoolisme chez la femme" ("Alcoholism among women"). La revue de l'alcoolisme 8: 289-291. [St Tr]

DeVAULT, B. M. (1965) "Women parolees. Parole performance of women referred to a mental health service unit." Crime and Delinquency 11: 272-282. [Co Tr]

DING, L. K. and L. Y. CHAN (1970) "A study of ex-prisoner female narcotic addicts in Hong Kong." Bull. on Narcotics, 22: 7-11. [Fo Pe St Tr]

DOLESCHAL, E. (1970) "The female offender: a guide to published materials." Crime and Delinquency Literature 2: 639-645. [Th]

d'ORBAN, P. T. (1973) "Female narcotic addicts: a follow-up study of criminal and addictions careers." British Medical J. 4: 345-347. [Fo St]

––– (1972a) "Baby stealing." British Medical J. 2: 635-639. [Ca Pe St Ty]

––– (1972b) "Female crime." Criminologist 7, 23: 29-51. [Co Pe So St]

––– (1971)"Social and psychiatric aspects of female crime." Medicine, Sci. and the Law 11: 104-116. [Co Pe So St]

EDWARDS, M. E. (1965) "Referral for social enquiry reports." Case Conference 12: 46-50. [Se]

ELLINWOOD, E. H., Jr., W. G. SMITH, and G. E. VAILLANT (1966) "Narcotic addiction in males and females: a comparison." International J. of the Addictions 1: 33-45. [Co Pe St]

ELLIS, D. P. and P. AUSTIN, (1971) "Menstruation and aggressive behavior in a correctional center for women." J. of Criminal Law, Criminology, and Police Sci. 62: 388-395. [So Tr]

ELMES, T. (1971) "Just like a woman." Police Rev. 79: 1271. [Co Th]

EVESON, M. (1967) "The female addict." The Canadian J. of Corrections 9: 227-233. [St Th]

––– (1964) "Research with female drug addicts at the prison for women." Canadian J. of Corrections 6: 21-27. [Pe St Tr]

EYMAN, J. S. (1966) "The myth of the father-image in women's prisons." Amer. J. of Corrections 28, 2: 10-11. [Tr]

EYSENCK, S.B.G. and H. J. EYSENCK (1973) "The personality of female prisoners." British J. of Psychiatry 123: 693-698. [Co Pe]

FAULKNER, D.E.R. (1971) "The redevelopment of Holloway prison." Howard J. of Penology and Crime Prevention 13: 122-132. [In]

FELICE, T. de (1963) "Au point de vue social, à quoi bon reclasser les prostituées?" ("From a social point of view, why re-educate the prostitute?"). Revue abolitionniste 88: 33-34. [St Th]

FLINT, M. S. (1964) "Narcotic addiction in women offenders." Canadian J. of Corrections 6: 246-265. [St Tr]

FORSLUND, M. A. (1970) "Standardization of negro crime rates for negro-white differences in age and status." Rocky Mountain Social Science J. 7: 151-160. [Co St]

FUJIWARA, T. (1966) "A psychiatric study of the prostitutes in Asakusa." Acta criminologiae et medicinae legalis japonica 32: 15-16. [Fo Pe St]

GAUPER, I. H. (1962) "Missouri state penitentiary for women." Amer. J. of Correction 24: 26-30. [In]

GEIS, G. and J. SOLER (1971) "Response of female homicide offenders to press coverage of their trials." Journalism Q. 48: 558-560. [Mi St]

GIALLOMBARDO, R. (1966) "Social roles in a prison for women." Social Problems 13: 268-288. [Co Tr]

GIANNELL, A. S. (1966) "Giannell's criminosynthesis theory applied to female homosexuality." J. of Psychology 64: 213-222. [Co Pe St]

GIBBENS, T.C.N., C. PALMER, and J. PRINCE (1971) "Mental health aspects of shoplifting." British Medical J. 3: 612-615. [Co Fo Pe So St]

GIBBS, C. (1971) "The effect of the imprisonment of women upon their children." British J. of Criminology 11: 113-130. [Mi]

GILLIES, H. (1965) "Murder in the west of Scotland." British J. of Psychiatry 111: 1087-1094. [Mi Pe St]

GREENBERG, H. R. (1966) "Pyromania in a woman." Psychoanalytic Q. 35: 256-262. [Ca Pe St]

GRIMBLE, A. (1965) "Morality and venereal disease." Excerpta criminologica 5: 383-406. [So St]

GROSHELL, C. P. (1964) "One woman's view of adult parole." Perspective 8: 2-3, 17. (International bibliography on crime and delinquency, 1965, 3: 410) [Th]

Groupe D'Etudes en Sociologie Juridique et Criminelle Gabriel-Tarde (1968) "Les comportements dissociaux" ("Dis-social behaviour"). Informations Sociales 22, 6: 82-88. [Th]

GUPTA, P. L. (1973) "Institutional and non-institutional services for rescued women and girls." Social Defence 8, 32: 19-23. [Pe St]

GUZE, S. B., R. A. WOODRUFF Jr., and P. J. CLAYTON (1971) "Hysteria and antisocial behavior: further evidence of an association." Amer. J. of Psychiatry 127: 957-960. [Co Pe]

HAMMER, M. (1969) "Hypersexuality in reformatory women." Corrective Psychiatry and J. of Social Therapy 15: 20-26. [Pe St Ty]
——— (1965) "Homosexuality in a women's reformatory." Corrective Psychiatry and J. of Social Therapy 11: 168-169. [Pe St]
HANNUM, T. E. and R. E. WARMAN (1964) "The MMPI characteristics of incarcerated females." J. of Research in Crime and Delinquency 1: 119-126. [Pe]
HANNUM, T. E., J. W. MENNE, E. L. BETZ, and L. RANS, (1973) "Differences in female prisoner characteristics — 1960 to 1970." Corrective and Social Psychiatry and J. of Applied Behavior Therapy 19, 3: 39-41. [Co Pe]
HARDER, T. (1967) "The psychopathology of infanticide." Acta psychiatrica scandinavica, 43: 196-245. [Ca Co Pe St]
HARTMAN, M. S. (1973) "Murder for respectability: the case of Madeleine Smith." Victorian Studies 16: 381-400. [Mi]
HASLAM, P. (1970) "The woman offender." Canadian J. of Corrections 12: 301-305. [Th]
——— (1964) "The female prisoner." Canadian J. of Corrections 6: 463-466. [In St]
——— (1963) "A house can be a home." Canadian J. of Corrections 5: 86-89. [In]
HEIDENSOHN, F. (1969) "Prison for women." Howard J. of Penology and Crime Prevention 12: 281-288. [Co In Tr]
——— (1968) "The deviance of women: a critique and an enquiry." British J. of Sociology 19: 160-175. [Th]
HEMMI, T. and Y. YABUKI (1964) "On female drug and alcoholic addicts." Acta criminologiae et medicinae legalis japonica 30: 13. [Pe St]
HENRY, B. C. (1974) "Helping women addicts at 'The Coke Hole,' England." International J. of Offender Therapy and Comp. Criminology 18: 68-76. [Ca In St Tr]
HIROSE, K. (1970) "A psychiatric study of female homicides. On the cases of parricide." Acta criminologiae et medicinae legalis japonica 36: 29. [Mi Pe St]
HIRSCHI, T. (1962) "The professional prostitute." Berkeley J. of Sociology 7: 33-50. [St Th]
HOBBS, D. B. and M. P. OSMAN (1967) "From prison to the community: a case study." Crime and Delinquency 13: 317-322. [Ca Tr]
HOFFMAN-BUSTAMANTE, D. (1973) "The nature of female criminality." Issues in Criminology 8, 2: 117-136. [Co St]

HOOPER, P.M.F. (1963) "Group work with Borstal girls." Howard J. of Penology and Crime Prevention 11: 119-133. [Tr]

HOROVITZ, M. (1964) Supplementary remarks to: H. Z. Winnik, "The psychopathology of infanticide: a case study." Israel Annals of Psychiatry and Related Disciplines 1: 306-309. [Ca]

HOVEY, M. (1971) "The forgotten offenders." Manpower (January): 38-41. (Crime and delinquency literature, 1972, 4: S9959) [St Tr]

ILIOPOULOS, C. and R. L. GATSKI (1961) "Fluphenazine treatment of behavioral disorders." Comprehensive Psychiatry 2: 364-367. [So Tr]

JACKMAN, N. R., R. O'TOOLE, and G. GEIS (1963) "The self-image of the prostitute." Sociological Q. 4: 150-161. [At Pe St]

JOAN ELIZABETH, Sister (1974) "Helping women addicts at Spelthorne St. Mary's, England." International J. of Offender Therapy and Comp. Criminology 18: 77-81. [St Tr]

JOHNSTON, W. C. (1968) "A descriptive study of 100 convicted female narcotic residents." Corrective Psychiatry and J. of Social Therapy 14: 230-236. [Pe St]

KAHN, M. W. (1971) "Murderers who plead insanity: a descriptive factor-analytic study of personality, social, and history variables." Genetic Psychology Monographs 84: 275-360. [Pe St]

KASSEBAUM, G. G., D. A. WARD, D. M. WILNER, and W. C. KENNEDY (1962) "Job related differences in staff attitudes toward treatment in a women's prison." Pacific Soc. Rev. 5: 83-88. [Mi]

KATRIN, S. E. (1974) "The effects on women inmates of facilitation training provided correctional officers." Criminal Justice and Behavior 1: 5-12. [Mi Pe Tr]

KAY, B. A. (1965) "Can you change this image? A report of male-female differences in attitude toward the police and legal institutions." Police 10, 2: 30-32. [At Co]

——— (1962) "Female prisoners; their concepts of self." Police 7, 2: 39-41. (International bibliography on crime and delinquency, 1963, 2: 563) [Pe]

KELLEY, J. E. (1970) "The new Holloway." Prison Service J. 10, 37: 2-8. [In]

——— and B. PAUL (1965) "Finding homes for homeless girls." Prison Service J. 4: 2-17. [Tr]

KETTERLING, M. E. (1970) "Rehabilitating women in jail." J. of Rehabilitation 36, 3: 36-38, 56. [Co Tr]

KING, P. (1964) "The woman inmate's contacts with the outside world." Amer. J. of Corrections 26, 3: 18-21. [In]

KLARE, H. J. (1969) "The institutional treatment of offenders." Medical and Biological Illustration 19: 142-145. [Co In]

KLEIN, D. (1973) "The etiology of female crime: a review of the literature." Issues in Criminology 8, 2: 3-30. [Pe]

KOCHER, M. B. (1961) "Tochigi women's prison, Japan." Correction 23: 20-25. (Excerpta criminologica, 1961, 1: 1608a) [In]

KOGI, S. and Y. ISHIKAWA (1961) "Sur la relation entre le crime ou le délit chez les femmes et leur menstruation—une considération psychiatrique et criminologique d'un cas de narcoleptique" ("The relation between crimes or offences by women and their menstruation—a psychiatric and criminological consideration of a case of narcolepsy"). Acta criminologiae et medicinae legalis japonica 27: 159-160. [So St]

KRAUSE, F. H., K. M. DIMICK, and R. E. HAYES (1972) "An itinerate psychological services program in a women's prison." Correctional Psychologist 5: 171-177. (Abstracts on criminology and penology, 1974, 14: 1375) [In Tr]

KREVELEN, D. A. van (1966) "Analysis of a prostitute." Acta paedopsychiatrica 33: 109-117. [Ca Pe St]

KUMAR, P. (1961) "Prostitution: a sociopsychological analysis." Indian J. of Social Work 21: 425-430. [Ca Pe St]

LANDREVILLE, P. (1969) "Population carcérale féminine au Canada" ("Female inmate population in Canada"). Revue canadienne de criminologie 11: 1-25. [Co Se St]

LANYON, R. I. (1969) "A personality scale for the assessment of criminality in women." Criminologica 6, 4: 33-39. [Co Pe]

LIBRANDI, F. L. (1968) "A mini-view of delinquent women." Bull. of the Society of Professional Investigators (October 24th): 18-21. (Abstracts on criminology and penology, 1969, 9: 1861) [St Th]

LINDSAY, M. K. (1970) "Prostitution—delinquency's time bomb." Crime and Delinquency, 16: 151-157. [In Se St Tr]

LORIMER, A. E. and M. HEADS (1962) "The significance of morale in a female penal institution." Federal Probation 26, 4: 38-44. [In Tr]

LUKIANOWICZ, N. (1971) "Infanticide." Psychiatria clinica 4: 145-158. [Ca Pe St Ty]

MAAS, J. P. (1966a) "Cathexes toward significant others by sociopathic women. Positive and negative distances." Archives of General Psychiatry 15: 516-522. [Pe]

——— (1966b) "The use of actional procedures in group psychotherapy with sociopathic women." The International Journal of Group Psychotherapy 16: 190-197. [Co Tr]

MALA, M. (1960) "Problems of women offenders of Nari Bandi Niketan, Lucknow." J. of Correctional Work 7: 85-91. [St Tr Ty]

MARTIN, J. E. and J. INGLIS (1965) "Pain tolerance and narcotic addiction." British J. of Social and Clinical Psychology 4: 224-229. [Co Pe St]

MATTHEW, J. R. (1964) "The female criminal sexual psychopath." Corrective Psychiatry and J. of Social Therapy 10: 156-158. [Ca Tr]

MAYER, J. and M. GREEN (1967) "Group therapy of alcoholic women ex-prisoners." Q. J. of Studies on Alcohol 28: 493-504. [St Tr]

MAYER, J., D. J. MYERSON, M. A. NEEDHAM, and M. M. FOX (1966) "The treatment of the female alcoholic: the former prisoner." Amer. J. of Orthopsychiatry 36: 248-249. [Co St Tr]

MAZLOUMAN, R. (1973) "Le 'crime d'honneur' Quelques articles du code pénal iranien" ("The 'crime d'honneur.' Some articles of the Iranian penal code"). Revue internationale de criminologie et de police technique 26: 38-40. [Th]

McCALDON, R. J. (1967) "Lady paperhangers." Canadian J. of Corrections 9: 243-256. [Ca Co Pe St]

McCLEAN, J. D. (1969) "Penal progress, 1968." Criminal Law Rev. (April): 167-177. [In]

McKERRACHER, D. W., D.R.K. STREET, and L. J. SEGAL (1966) "A comparison of the behaviour problems presented by male and female subnormal offenders." British J. of Psychiatry 112: 891-897. [Co Pe Tr]

MERRICK, B. (1970) "Shoplifting—a microcosm." Criminologist 5, 18: 68-81. [St]

METZ, B. H. (1967) "Alienation among female probationers." J. of the California Probation, Parole and Correction Assn. 4: 37-45. [Co Pe]

MEYER, A. (1961) "La prostitution, fléau social" ("Prostitution, a social scourge"). Revue internationale de police criminelle 16: 22-25. [St Th]

MILLER, E. E. (1969) "The woman participant in Washington's riots." Federal Probation 33, 2: 30-34. [In Pe St Ty]

MILLER, W. G. and T. E. HANNUM (1963) "Characteristics of homosexually involved incarcerated females." J. of Consulting Psychology 27: 277. [Co Pe St]

MILSTEIN, F. (1971) "Special problems in treating female offenders: clarifying the patient's sense of identity." International J. of Offender Therapy 15: 16-20. [Ca Pe Tr]

MINNIS, M. S. (1963) "Prostitution and social class: as viewed in recent popular literature." Proceedings of the Southwestern Sociological Association 13: 1-6. (Soc. Abstracts, 1964, 12: B3006) [Tr]

MOGAL, D. P. (1969) "A research project in teaching in a women's prison." Community Mental Health J. 5: 247-255. [Tr]

MONTAGUE, M. E. (1963) "Women prisoners respond to contemporary dance." J. of Health, Physical Education, Recreation 34, 3: 25-26, 74. [Ca Mi]

MORGAN, A. M. (1964) "Women in preventive detention." Prison Service J. 4: 11-25. [Co Pe Tr]

MURPHY, K. M. and R. Y. D'ANGELO (1963) "The intelligence factor in the criminality of women." Amer. Catholic Soc. Rev. 24: 340-347. [Pe]

MYERSON, D. J. (1959) "Clinical observations on a group of alcoholic prisoners—with special reference to women." Q. J. of Studies on Alcohol 20: 555-572. [Pe St]

NAGEL, S. and L. J. WEITZMAN (1972) "Double standard of American justice." Society 9, 5: 18-25, 62-63. [Co Se]

National Association of Probation Officers (1966) "Supervision of women and girls." Probation 12: 94-96. [Tr]

NEWBERG, P. M. (1967) "The female of the species: a systematic review of theories, evaluations and studies of the female criminal." Interdiscipline 4: 29-42. [Th]

O'MALLEY, E. P. and H. BLUESTONE (1965) "Trials and tribulations in conducting a drug study in a women's prison." Psychosomatics 6: 95-99. [So St]

O'REILLY, C., F. CIZON, J. FLANAGAN, and S. PFLANCZER (1968) "Sentenced women in a county jail." Amer. J. of Correction 30, 2: 23-25. [St]

OSTRANDER, M. R. (1963) "The female offender." Law and Order 11: 40-41, 70-73. (Excerpta criminologica, 1964, 4: 1034) [Pe Ty]

PARKER, M. C. (1968) "After institutionalization." Canadian J. of Corrections 10: 432-437. [Tr]

PAYAK, B. J. (1963) "Understanding the female offender." Federal Probation 27, 4: 7-12. [Pe Th]

PEIRCE, F. J. (1963) "Social group work in a women's prison." Federal Probation 27, 4: 37-43. [Tr]

PERRIE, O. (1964) "Group work in a girls' borstal." Prison Service J. 3: 44-46. [Tr]

PFOUTS, J. and Q. D. MEYER (1961) "Examination of a sample of inmates in a southern women's prison." Correction 23: 7-12. (Excerpta Criminologica, 1961, 1: 1608) [Pe]

PRASHAD, U. (1973) "Rehabilitation of women rescued from moral danger." Social Defence 8, 32: 4-10. [St Tr]

QUARLES, M. S. (1964) "How one woman's reformatory interests students in the correctional field." Amer. J. of Correction 26, 3: 32-35. [In]

RAPPEPORT, J. R. and G. LASSEN (1966) "The dangerousness of female patients: a comparison of the arrest rate of discharged psychiatric patients and the general population." Amer. J. of Psychiatry 123: 413-419. [Co St]

REINCKE, F. G. (1965) "Connecticut's correctional institutions." Amer. J. of Corrections 27, 4: 30-32. [In]

ROBIN, G. D. (1963) "Patterns of department store shoplifting." Crime and Delinquency 9: 163-172. [Co St]

ROBINSON, B. F. (1961) "Criminality among narcotic addicts in the Illinois state reformatory for women." Illinois Medical J. 119: 320-326. [Pe St]

ROSENBLATT, E. and C. GREENLAND (1974) "Female crimes of violence." Canadian J. of Criminology and Corrections 16: 173-180. [Co St]

ROSENBLATT, G. F. and T. E. HANNUM (1969) "Relationship between Machiavellianism and sociopathy in an incarcerated female population." Correctional Psychologist 3: 16-22. (Abstracts on criminology and penology, 1970, 10: 1265) [Pe]

ROSS, H. L. (1959) "The 'hustler' in Chicago." J. of Student Research 1: 13-19. [St]

ROTNER, S. (1963) "Design for a women's prison: an architect's view." The Howard J. 11: 134-144. [In]

RUBIN, L. (1968) "The racist liberals—an episode in a county jail." Transaction 5: 39-44. [In Th]

SANDHU, H. S. and L. H. IRVING (1974) "Female offenders and marital disorganisation: an aggressive and retreatist reaction." International J. of Criminology and Penology 2: 35-42. [Co Pe]

SANNITO, T. C. and T. E. HANNUM (1966) "Relationship between the WAIS and indices of sociopathy in an incarcerated female population." J. of Research in Crime and Delinquency 3: 63-70. [Pe]

SCHMIDEBERG, M. (1971) "Special problems in treating female offenders: promiscuous and rootless girls." International J. of Offender Therapy 15: 28-33. [Pe]

SIMMONS, I. L. and J. W. ROGERS (1970) "The relationship between type of offense and successful postinstitutional adjustment of female offenders." Criminologica 7, 4: 68-76. [Co Fo St]

SINGER, L. R. (1973) "Women and the correctional process." Amer. Criminal Law Rev. 11: 295-308. (Abstracts on criminology and penology, 1973, 13: 2526) [Th]

SINGH, U. P. (1972) "Comparative study of attitudes of male and female criminals towards their family, parents and authority." J. of the Indian Academy of Applied Psychology 9: 18-21. [At Co]

SLATER, A. L. (1961) "Infanticide—report of two cases." Medical J. of Australia, 1: 819-821. [Ca Pe St]

SLOVENKO, R. (1964) "Are women more law-abiding than men?" Police 8, 6: 17-24. (Excerpta criminologica, 1965, 5: 365) [Co Se]

SMITH, A. D. (1969) "The treatment of women offenders." British J. of Criminology 9: 396-398. [Th]

——— (1965) "Penal policy and the woman offender." Soc. Rev. Monograph 9: Soc. Studies in the British Penal Services, 111-132. [Se St]

SNORTUM, J. R., T. E. HANNUM, and D. H. MILLS (1970) "The relationship of self-concept and parent image to rule violations in a women's prison." J. of Clinical Psychology 26: 284-287. [Pe Tr]

SOHIER, J. (1969) "A rather ordinary crime: shoplifting." International Criminal Police Rev. 24: 161-166. [St Th]

STANG, H. J. (1967) "A diagnostic and prognostic study of a material comprising abnormal Norwegian delinquents." Acta psychiatrica scandinavica 43: 111-120. [Co Fo Pe]

STEFANOWICZ, J. P. and T. E. HANNUM (1971) "Ethical risk-taking and sociopathy in incarcerated females." Correctional Psychologist 4: 138-152. (Psych. Abstracts, 1972, 48: 5249) [Pe]

STERNLICHT, M. (1966) "Treatment approaches to delinquent retardates." International J. of Group Psychotherapy 16: 91-93. [Tr]

STOFFER, S. S., J. D. SAPIRA, and B. F. MEKETON (1969) "Behavior in ex-addict female prisoners participating in a research study." Comprehensive Psychiatry 10: 224-232. [Pe So St Tr]

STURGES, T. (1965) "Experiment in Holloway: a new approach to prison visiting." Prison Service J. 4: 22-29. [In]

SUAREZ, J. M., V. G. HADDOX, and H. MITTMAN (1972) "The establishment of a therapeutic community within a women's correctional facility." J. of Forensic Sci. 17: 561-567. [Tr]

SUTKER, P. B. and C. E. MOAN (1973) "A psychosocial description of penitentiary inmates." Archives of General Psychiatry 29: 663-667. [Co Pe]

SUVAL, E. M. and R. C. BRISSON (1974) "Neither beauty nor beast: female criminal homicide offenders." International J. of Criminology and Penology 2: 23-34. [Co Pe St]

TAKAHASHI, R., K. MARUYAMA, and S. ODA (1966) "A criminal case of craniopharyngioma." Acta criminologiae et medicinae legalis japonica 32: 13 [Ca So]

TASKAR, K. T. (1960) "Recidivism among women." Indian Sociologist 2: 14-18. (Soc. Abstracts, 1964, 12: B2243) [Co Pe St]

TAYLOR, A.J.W. (1968) "A search among Borstal girls for the psychological and social significance of their tattoos." British J. of Criminology 8: 170-185. [Co Pe So]

––– (1967) "An evaluation of group psychotherapy in a girls' borstal." International J. of Group Psychotherapy 17: 168, 177. [Co Fo Pe Tr]

––– (1965) "The significance of 'darls' or 'special relationships' for Borstal girls." British J. of Criminology 5: 406-418. [Pe Tr]

TENNENT, T. G., A. McQUAID, T. LOUGHNANE, and A. J. HANDS (1971) "Female arsonist." British J. of Psychiatry 119: 497-502. [Co Pe St]

THOMPSON, G. R. (1968) "Institutional programs for female offenders." Canadian J. of Corrections 10: 438-441. [Tr]

TOMORUG, E., I. VERNEA, V. SRIBU, and S. BAZILESCU (1963) "Psychoses de la maternité et criminalité. Psychoses dites puerpérales" ("Post-partum psychoses and criminality. So-called puerperal psychoses"). Acta medicinae legalis et socialis 16: 47-56. [Ca Pe So]

TOTMAN, J. (1971) "The murderess." Police 15, 6: 16-22. [St Th]

TRAINI, R. (1972) "Cherchez la femme. Increased participation in crime by women poses problems of detection." Security Gazette 14: 352-353. [Th]

Troisième réunion internationale des chefs des administrations pénitentiaires, Lisbonne, 22-27 septembre (1969) Revue de droit pénal et de criminologie 50: 145-147. [Tr]

TUTEUR, W. and J. GLOTZER (1966) "Further observations on murdering mothers." J. of Forensic Sciences 11: 373-383 (Crime and delinquency abstracts, 1966, 4: 5886). [Mi Pe St]

––– (1959) "Murdering mothers." Amer. J. of Psychiatry 116: 447-452. [Ca Pe St]

ULMER, W. F. (1965) "History of Maine correctional institutions." Amer. J. of Corrections 27, 4: 33-35. [In]

VAN HAECHT, A. (1972) "Image et statut de la prostituée–Essai d'intégration de la prostitution dans le systéme social global." Revue de droit pénal et de criminologie 52: 853-881. [St Th]

VERSELE, S. C. (1969) "Study of female shoplifters in department stores." International Criminal Police Rev. 24: 66-70. [Pe St]

VESTERGAARD, E. and G. MORTENSSON (1963) "Psychiatric examination of young female prostitutes." International Criminal Police Rev. 18: 76-80. [Pe St Ty]

WALLACH, A. and L. RUBIN (1971-1972) "The premenstrual syndrome and criminal responsibility." UCLA Law Rev. 19: 209-312. [Se So]

WARD, D. A. and G. G. KASSEBAUM (1964) "Homosexuality: a mode of adaptation in a prison for women." Social Problems 12: 159-177. [Co St Tr]

WARMAN, R. E. and T. E. HANNUM (1965a) "MMPI pattern changes in female prisoners." J. of Research in Crime and Delinquency 2: 72-76. [Pe]

––– (1965b) "Use of parole violators in pre-parole group counseling." Corrective Psychiatry and J. of Social Therapy 11: 269-274. [Tr]

WEBB, A. P. and P. V. RILEY (1970) "Effectiveness of casework with young female probationers." Social Casework 51: 566-572. [Co Fo Pe Tr]

WEIS, K. and S. S. BORGES (1973) "Victimology and rape: the case of the legitimate victim." Issues in Criminology 8, 2: 71-115. [Mi]

WEITMAN, M. (1963) "Extent of criminal activity, sex, and varieties of authoritarianism." Psych. Reports 13: 217-218. [At Co]

WINNIK, H. Z. (1963) "The psychopathology of infanticide: a case study." Israel Annals of Psychiatry and Related Disciplines 1: 293-306. [Ca Pe St Tr]

––– and M. HOROVITZ (1961) "The problem of infanticide." British J. of Criminology 2: 40-52. [Pe St]

Woman goes to prison (a) (1963). Out and About,1, 14-17. (International bibliography on crime and delinquency, 1964, 2:00767) [At Ca]

Women Endorsing Decriminalization (1973) "Prostitution: a non-victim crime?" Issues in Criminology 8, 2: 137-162. [St Th]

WOODFIELD, P. (1970) "Chronique anglaise" ("English chronicle"). Revue pénitentiaire et de droit pénal 70: 65-70. [Tr]

WOODSIDE, M. (1963) "Attitudes of women abortionists." The Howard J. 11: 93-112. [At St]

––– (1962a) "Instability in women prisoners." Lancet 2: 928-930. [Ca Pe]

––– (1962b) "Profile of a prison population: sentence and social background of 890 women in Holloway prison, 1959-1960." Prison Service J. 2: 26-42. [Pe St]

––– (1961) "Women drinkers admitted to Holloway prison during February 1960: a pilot survey." British J. of Criminology 1: 221-235. [St]

YADA, S. and O. FUNAKI (1965) "Infanticide by multiple cut wounds."
  Acta criminologiae et medicinae legalis japonica 31: 78-79. [Ca Mi St]
YOSHIMASU, S., N. TAKEMURA, and T. TSUBOI (1959) "A study on
  criminal process of female recidivist." Japanese J. of Criminal Law 9:
  208-220. (Psych. Abstracts, 1960, 34: 6339) [Co Pe]
ZIETZ, D. (1963) "Child welfare services in a women's correctional
  institution." Child Welfare 42: 185-190. [In Tr]

Selections from the Proceedings of the Third Alabama
Symposium on Justice and the Behavioral Sciences

INTRODUCTION

It is difficult to seek out information about programs and research for
females in corrections. The neglect and apathy that characterize the
professional response to females and justice led us to organize a conference
at the University of Alabama in January 1974, devoted to planning for the
female offender. The conference was designed to promote the exchange of
information and ideas, to advance our present state of knowledge, and to
provide impetus for creative program development. This section of the
special journal issue contains edited proceedings of that conference.

The selections here represent input from women outside the criminal
justice system, such as Wilma Scott Heide, president of the National
Organization for Women, and input from women with experience and
expertise within the system, such as Martha Wheeler, past president of the
American Correctional Association. The other papers represent different
avenues of intervention into the system by professionals. Virginia
Pendergrass offers the perspective of a private practitioner who works as a
volunteer in the criminal justice system; Eileen Slack represents the
professional as an administrator of an institution; and Farris Lawrence
provides the input of the ex-offender who has been the recipient of the
services of the criminal justice system.

The extent to which female offenders have difficulty making their
specific needs known has been reflected in the professional literature, with
its minimal focus on female-related problems of offenders; rather articles
typically focus more broadly on offenders in general. Perhaps it will be left

to feminists outside of corrections to point the way to recognition and reform of problems specific to females. As Ms. Wheeler pointed out, those in corrections who have the experience and expertise do not traditionally record and report their impressions. This leaves others to interpret the situation either from work applied to males, or data based on very little knowledge of women in corrections.

In this light, the next steps are twofold: first, a research effort to amass the missing data from our knowledge of female offenders; second, an effort to encourage citizen and community participation. Corrections must begin to respond to the needs of this relatively quiet minority in the criminal justice system.

—Annette M. Brodsky

INNOVATIVE PROGRAMS FOR WOMEN IN JAIL AND PRISONS
Trick or Treatment

VIRGINIA E. PENDERGRASS
Department of Social Work
Florida International University

It is clear that there is no lack of important, reasonable, and innovative approaches to problems faced by women in jail and prison which eventually, with research and experimental application, must lead to significant progress. Vocational training, behavior modification, transactional analysis, family therapy from psychology; pretrial intervention and work release from the legal and social work fields; and youth programs from education are only a few possibilities. All that is needed is big money for implementation of research and application.

However most "innovative programs" for women in jail and prison mean developing clever little ideas using volunteers (i.e., unpaid women) which do not cost money, because we are not providing the money and personpower necessary to implement important, truly innovative programs for women. Programs for women in jail which adjust to pitifully meager funding and exploit women as volunteers are indeed a trick, not a treatment. We are all aware that conviction of a crime does not necessarily proceed from having committed the crime; one is rather convicted because one is poor, a minority group member, and also guilty (Bagdikian and Dash, 1972). Programs which do not change this are a trick. They are a trick when the helping hand offered to the selected individual inmate corrodes the unity of the oppressed group. They are a trick when they generate favorable publicity and stimulate good citizens to feel that "everything humanly possible is being done to help those poor unfortunates." They are a trick when the social and economic system generating the situations of these women in jail and prison does not change.

The present paper discusses two innovative approaches to women in the criminal justice system designed to subvert clever little programs using volunteers: (1) a program to put people in decision-making positions who will use their influence to generate funding and use their authority to implement important programs; and (2) programs to teach female inmates how to appreciate themselves, expect fair treatment, and use their power to gain fair treatment when it is denied.

Putting people in decision-making positions. Until 1972, women prisoners in Dade County were kept in a corner of one floor of the Dade County Jail, a predominantly male institution. Their principal activity was sewing, and they were greatly restricted in moving from one area of the jail to another for visits or recreation because they needed an escort in order to pass through the male sections of the jail. For the same reason, women were not allowed to participate in in-house work programs.

In 1971-1972, a series of exposes of the Dade County Jail appeared in the Miami *Herald.* As a result of these news stories, a "Committee of 100" irate, private, but prominent citizens, mostly women, was formed. They regularly visited the jail and pressed for change in the system, and also cooperated with the very critical mass media in a continuing condemnation of the jail. At the end of 1971, county public officials were feeling very hard-pressed and persecuted by the community and the media. At the same time, planning for the 1972 Democratic and Republican conventions began.

One of the expectations of the county officials was that there might be numerous arrests related to civil disturbances during the convention, and extra space in the county jail would be needed. To supply this, a City of Miami facility was transferred to the county, and the women in the Dade County Jail were moved to the new unit, which became the Dade County Female Detention Center.

In ignorance of these machinations, the Dade County Chapter of the National Organization for Women (Dade County NOW) sent their Task Force on Women in Jail to the offices of the county manager and the director of the Dade County Jail to demand a facility for women and a female director of that facility. The task force was astounded to be received in the county manager's office by a panel of representatives with pen in hand, ready to take notes. They were amazed to meet with the director of the jail and be assured that a female unit would be created, as well as to discover that new vocational programs in typing, cosmetology, and high school equivalency training would be planned. The task force was asked to recommend women who might be qualified for the position of director of the Women's Detention Center.

As they canvassed the nation for women candidates, it became clear that the director of the Dade County Jail was not committed to an intensive search, and wanted to hire or promote someone he knew in the Dade County area. The task force, therefore, supplied the names of a number of local candidates, one of whom was personally known to the director as a former policewoman. She had since completed a Ph.D. in psychology and counseled with delinquent girls in a youth center in the area. She was selected as the new director of the Women's Detention Center.

During the course of the following year, the task force followed up this appointment by visits to the county manager's office and the director of the jail to insure continuation of the candidate in the office. The results of this appointment were:

(1) The NOW Task Force was allowed to meet regularly in the Women's Detention Center with female inmates representing each dormitory cell.

(2) The director of the Women's Detention Center implemented the proposed typing and cosmetology courses, as well as group

counseling for drug abusers, and responded to requests for special college-level programs for inmates and professionals offered through Florida International University and Miami-Dade Community College.

(3) She began systematic data collection specifically on women inmates, and freely provided information to local groups.

(4) She was selected to represent Dade County on a statewide board which monitors dispensation of funds and management of the entire penal system in Florida.

On the basis of this experience, it is now clear that one of the most powerful change agents in a sorry social system is a highly principled, intelligent, and sympathetic person in an executive position, who can provide information to activists, who can present good programs at high-level boards and governmental meetings, and who can approve good programs for inmates and personnel under her/his supervision.

Although in Dade County the placement of a highly principled, intelligent, and sympathetic person of NOW's choice in the position of director of the Female Detention Center was a more or less chance event, it seems reasonable that an analogous deliberate action plan could lead to the same result. The plan might read as follows:

(1) News media and radical groups should be encouraged to demonstrate, expose, criticize, and otherwise put public pressure on the criminal justice system;

(2) Key positions in the criminal justice system, in terms of responsibility, supervision, or access to information, should be identified, and longevity of each executive evaluated by these criteria:

(a) is the person approaching retirement?

(b) is the person ambitious and likely to be mobile?

(c) is the person highly respected or is her/his competence questioned publicly?

(d) is the job complex enough to warrant creation of a new position to handle part of the duties of the executive on an equal level?

(3) When a likely position is identified, a request should be made by a respectable, but active, group of citizens, preferably not identified with those "troublemakers" who generated the bad publicity, regarding employment of a particular type of person;

(4) The request should clearly specify qualifications, which might include sex, race, academic background, social science orientation, and the like;

(5) When an executive position becomes available, names of selected individuals who fill the previously submitted description should be provided;

(6) Appointments should be followed up by expressions of approval and estimations of progress, especially if the new executive is experiencing difficulties due to innovations.

Teaching self-determination to inmates and personnel. When a clever, little (free) program using women volunteers is initiated, the objective of the volunteers should be to build solidarity between inmates, not separate inmates by selecting out and encouraging identification with authority. Furthermore, the programs should provide information and techniques which might lead the inmates to develop their own programs and use appropriate community resources as allies in political pressure. Two programs in Dade County which had potential in this way were the "legal rap" and "women's medical self-help." Each had the potential of building participant confidence and information, relieving deep anxieties, and preparing participants for effective action. Neither was entirely successful.

The NOW Task force on Women in Jail, with the permission of the new director of the Women's Detention Center, met at the detention center once a month. Their first objective was to have more female lawyers hired by the department of public defense, and to have the female public defenders assigned to female inmates, rather than juvenile court, the usual assignment. The vociferous approval of the female inmates was somewhat of a surprise, since employment and promotion of female lawyers appeared to be a primarily middle-class concern. The women inmates indicated, however, that they had many concerns about health, family, and other very personal matters that they felt reluctant to discuss with a man. The women also stated that they felt that a woman could better understand the woman's situation, and be a more determined and sympathetic defender in court.

The NOW Task Force, including the women selected from the cells to represent the inmates, prepared a survey of public defense services and the inmate members administered the survey to the women in their own sections. They also made an attempt to analyze the results, and prepared a preliminary report. The final report, written by NOW members, included letters generated by the women in the detention center supporting the plan.

The results of the survey showed that 50% of the women saw their public defenders for fifteen minutes or less, and that more than half did not know the name of their public defender. Of the women who saw public defenders for more than fifteen minutes, most were accused of a capital crime, in which case the usual interview length was one to one and one-half hours. At this point, the irrelevancy of asking for female public defenders instead of male defenders became clear. The final plan of action was presented to the public defender's office, with copies to the county manager's office and the director of the Women's Detention Center, by a joint committee of NOW members and female inmates serving on the NOW Task Force.

The requests for action read as follows:

(1) All public defenders who are assigned to represent an inmate shall give a typewritten slip of paper, signed, to each inmate with name and telephone number and date of first interview, so that the inmates may contact the defender after initial interviews, if necessary;

(2) An inmate training program shall be instituted in two parts:

(a) the public defender's office shall provide a lawyer, public or private, who will hold one hour seminars each week at the jail to discuss legal questions with inmates (the "legal rap");

(b) the public defenders shall begin to train selected inmates to carry out comprehensive interviews according to interview forms provided by the public defender's office;

(3) The public defender's office shall prepare a proposal, within one year, with outline for funding, to institute a paralegal system to support overworked public defenders in their duties;

(4) The public defender's office shall prepare an affirmative action program to hire female public defenders in accordance with national legislation against discrimination on the basis of sex (Commerce Clearing House, 1972). The plan should include:

(a) special recruiting presentations to female legal societies about career opportunities in public defense;

(b) special recruitment to include female students in volunteer and training programs in public defense;

(c) special advertising indicating that the Office of the Dade County Public Defender is a nondiscriminatory equal employer, pointing out opportunities to minorities and women in government service;

(d) cooperation with the law association and colleges and universities in locating qualified female applicants;

(5) The Public Defender's office shall urge appointment of women to the Penal Reform Committee of the Florida Bar Association and the Legal Aid and Indigent Defendant Committee of the Florida Bar Association.

The "legal rap" was considered to be one of the most significant elements of the program. Women's experience in the movement has shown that supportive group discussions which provide information and speak to women's deepest anxieties and needs (consciousness-raising) are essential prerequisites to action. The most salient anxieties of women in jail are the meaning of charges filed against them, what the public defender can do, and how the court system works. Correctional officers who counsel women on personal or family problems are not allowed to give legal information, and questions continually occur, long after the brief single interview with the public defender.

As a result of this petition, when hiring of public defenders which had been in progress was completed, several female trainees were accepted and assigned to the Women's Detention Center, and legal raps were initiated. The female inmates responded so favorably that the same practice was transferred to the male inmates' facilities.

The NOW Task Force over time waned in activity through loss of several responsible and active volunteers who responded to other commitments. One year later, all of the female inmates who originally participated in the Task Force were gone, the social workers who had represented the administration were either promoted or transferred, and the NOW members had maintained only a superficial contact with the detention center. A recent check showed that the entire idea of the legal rap had been lost, and that the public defenders now used the rap time for the individual 15-minute interviews with inmates who requested such an interview.

An analysis of this experiment produces one obvious con-clusion—volunteers cannot accept continuing, sustained respon-sibility for ongoing projects, and should therefore plan spot actions which include training of others to pick up on the program. Although the rap was very successful during its term, the jail personnel were obviously not aware of the important elements or the concept of the program. When the leadership inspiring the action was gone, the rap reverted to the traditional activity understood by public defenders and personnel as their responsibility. A more appropriate role for the task force might have been to teach public defenders and jail personnel the rap concept and train a number of individuals in good leading of small group discussion. More emphasis should also no doubt have been placed on ensuring that the women involved in the gathering of data and confrontation of the public defenders understood techniques of gathering information, the persuasive importance of good information, and elements of effective confrontation.

The second program of interest was a slide presentation by two women founders of the Women's Medical Self-Help Clinics

(The Monthly Extract) in California. The slide show included frames demonstrating self-examination and showing a number of common conditions one might observe, such as changes in the cervix during pregnancy, effects of birth control pills on coloration of the cervix, the string of an IUD and the usual drainage associated with it, small sores of veneral disease, and so forth. The dialogue during the program gave in simple, clear terms information on venereal disease, birth control, pregnancy, minor infections, and in addition presented a strongly positive attitude toward women's bodies.

The program was concluded by an in vivo demonstration of self-examination, and the participants were invited to do self-examination themselves. Most of the inmates in fact did so, and found the experience very rewarding. The detention center infirmary was provided with specula, flashlight, and mirror for self-examination, and several women have since requested permission to perform a self-examination during routine first aid treatment.

This program was of special significance primarily because of the strong feelings of pride and appreciation of one's own body that were conveyed. In addition, however, its medical significance was important. The detention center does not perform regular physical examinations on women entering the jail, although it is well known that venereal disease is common among the inmate population and that venereal disease is somewhat difficult to detect in women. A recent survey of thirteen inmates with a history of prostitution admitted in a two-week period showed that every woman except one had a history of "sex infections." There is some question about whether homosexual contacts communicate venereal disease as readily as heterosexual contacts. Recent interviews in Miami with gay couples have revealed very low incidence of venereal disease. If homosexual activity does communicate venereal disease, however, then by inmate reports of extensive homosexual activity one can only conclude that venereal disease is rampant in the detention center.

Medical care in general, and gynecological care in particular, for poor, minority women is inadequate at best. In the jail, it is almost nonexistent. Education of the women about their own bodies and preparation of them to understand their needs appears to be a preliminary step to protest about health care in jail and out.

Again, this volunteer program was a one-shot effort, and did not include elements of organization of inmates and/or jail personnel, preparation of information, and effective protest action. The self-help program, therefore, at this point is a rather fond memory of a few inmates and jail personnel.

CONCLUSION

Both of these programs failed in their full potential, but both prepared the way for effective action. At this point, the NOW Task Force is ready to work in the Women's Detention Center again. Much thought will be given to teaching inmates and sympathetic personnel the concepts, research techniques, data analysis techniques, reporting methods, use of mass media and volunteer groups for political pressure, and confrontation techniques which will encourage bonding of women in jail and prison to one another, and which will enable each woman to organize her own protest wherever she is.

REFERENCES

BAGDIKIAN, B. H. and L. DASH (1972) The Shame of the Prisons. New York: Pocket Books.

Commerce Clearing House (1972) "New 1972 equal employment opportunity law with explanation." Labor Law Reports 1: 293. (whole extra edition)

Women's Medical Self-Help Clinics (irregular periodical) The Monthly Extract: Stamford, Conn.: New Moon Publications.

FEMINISM AND
THE "FALLEN WOMAN"

WILMA SCOTT HEIDE
Past President, National Organization for Women
Visting Scholar, University of Massachusetts
Guest in Residence, Wellesley College

The title of this conference is "Planning for the Female Offender," and judging from the conference participants, indeed, it may be not only planning for, but planning with. I consider this very important for many reasons—among them, if people can be a part of the planning, people are more likely to accept the consequences of the planning.

The use of the term offender as the identification of a person at any point in time is troublesome. Very often those who have been identified and have been convicted as offenders of our society and its laws have themselves been victimized and learned very well how to victimize others and themselves. It might be accurate to say in relation to the "fallen woman" that *if* ever she was "fallen," she was politically and semantically pushed or shoved a good deal of the way. In relation to women in general as a class or caste of people, hopefully now she has risen, thanks to the rebirth of feminism by feminists, which generally needs defining.

A feminist believes that women, just as men, are primarily people. It is the commonality that all human beings share, and it is a transcending reality. A feminist believes that human rights must become indivisible by any category whether it be by sex, by race, by national origin, by creed—whatever. These are parts of our identity. Our totality is greater than any part. Furthermore, a feminist is committed to creating the kind of society and world where human rights are indivisible and where women and men, girls and boys have really equal rights and responsibilities in every aspect of life, in and outside the home—legally, politically, economically, religiously, and in every aspect of life. We consider that an absolute basic necessity for any kind of a fully human family and humane people. Feminism is central to humanism.

If indeed women who are feminists were really anti-men, as some folks allege, I can assure you what we would be doing is perpetuating and accelerating the status quo. Males start out life as constitutionally the weaker organism of the two sexes; they are subject to more serious and severe illnesses. The nature of our society is disadvantageous to those men who are victims of the masculine mystique and play the "masculinity" game, particularly in its more negative aspects. They are so pressed to perform in and outside of the bedroom, and these stresses are of such a nature and to such an extent that men die on the average of six to seven years younger than women. If we were anti-men, we would not be involved in transcending the limitations of the masculinity and the femininity games.

Women have been expected to be the moral arbiters of either real or alleged standards. There are those who believe that women are by nature morally superior to men. I do not support that theory. I do believe that our conditioning has required us to be more pro-life than has been permitted for most men. But if we were indeed so morally superior, it seems to me that we would be forced to be the religionists and be the leaders of not only our religious institutions but also our educational, political, and economic institutions. The symbol of justice in the United States is the blindfolded woman. Among other things, we are removing the blindfold to balance the scales of justice.

At NOW's recent national conference in Washington, we symbolically took over the Supreme Court. We simulated the Supreme Court, with a table, gavel, and a case decided by the nine women on our supreme court. The case was brought by a man as a class action on behalf of all men. The issue was that it was in their view unconstitutional to expect men to obey laws that were made solely or primarily by women, interpreted and judged solely or primarily by women.

There has never been a constitutional test of whether or not women really should be expected to obey laws in which we have had little or no part in the writing, enforcement, and interpretation. Revolutions have been fought for lesser reasons for a lesser number of people. The idea of no taxation without adequate representation must remain alive. This means women's equal representation in the courts, on the police, on commissions, in Congress, in the executive branches of government at every level, and in the administration of corrections with both women and men as administrators in the instance that both women and men have been defined as offenders.

Just as we have had taxation with little or no representation, we also find that some people have more representation than their inadequate taxation according to their resources should warrant. Most of the poor in this country, by anyone's definition—including the figures of the Department of Labor, Department of Commerce, and Census Bureau (and assuredly, these people are not yet feminists)—indicate that unemployment, underemployment, poverty, by whatever the current definition, is visited mostly on women and dependent children, and disproportionately on minority women.

We look at the United Fund that presumably serves people, and we find that, on the average, twice as much is given for men's and boys' organizations and activities as for women's and girls'. This is one of many reasons why we simply say, "We refuse to give our money to something that perpetuates sexism" in terms of the role assignments within the United Fund's agencies and in terms of the allocations of funds.

It is quite interesting in this particular administration in Washington that at the same time funds for health, education, welfare, housing, as well as other programs in the area of social services, were illegally impounded, we saw the emergence of the administration's support for volunteer centers for action. Have you seen the poster that says, "What these people need (and there is a picture of somebody who for one reason or another is indicated to have some need) money can't buy. They need you." We disagree. What these people need, money *can* buy. If we value these services at all, we have to value them enough to give the public funds to provide them.

In the whole volunteer effort of people in this country, most of the volunteers are women. NOW has taken a position and some subsequent action in this regard. Most of what we need is an educational effort. I and every other officer of NOW, as well as most of our members, are volunteers. It was only within the last year and a half that we have been able to have any staff at all. It is only within the last year or two that we have had our expenses reimbursed, and that only for a relative few of us so that we do not go bankrupt. We are not opposed to volunteerism per se. Some of the most significant things that have ever been done in this or any other country have been done by volunteers committed to the courage of their convictions. We do believe that we have to take a whole look at volunteerism and what it does. It of course perpetuates the feminine mystique. It makes the assumption that women have men to provide for them. It provides for further divisions (of which we need no more) of people at different income levels. And it causes resentment, particularly among people who can't afford to volunteer, but who need many of the jobs which volunteers can sometimes afford to take. So we have a situation where multiple standards exist in our society.

When women, whether girls or adults, come in contact with the law, they may be incarcerated not because they have really violated a law but because they have violated social norms. We have the still current phenomenon of women being protected and therefore incarcerated presumably for their own good. One of the things we are saying is, "Protect us from any more protectors." As women are considered sick, led astray, or misguided, we see in the criminal justice system that women are not always taken seriously. In the minds of some, it might be an advantage, because women may be let off mildly whereas a man committing the same offense may get the full punishment of the law. Judges may be reluctant to sentence women. Yet, if they do, it is still possible in some states that women may receive longer sentences for the same offense as that committed by men. The "rationale" presumably is that it is more abhorrent for a woman to violate the law or to do things that are considered immoral than it is for a man. And therefore, to teach them a lesson, women must have the longer sentence. That's one reason the Constitutional Equal Rights Amendment must be ratified to equalize the legal rights of women and men.

NOW has been instrumental in persuading the American Civil Liberties Union to have a women's rights project that has included some information to women about their rights in general and their rights as prisoners. Some of our chapters are about to have a chapter of NOW in a prison in the northern part of California. We do consciousness-raising with those who are "offenders" in the prisons and with the staffs.

One of the most important things that we can do for and with women in jail and within the criminal justice system is to teach more assertive behavior. We must do so for our own self-confidence and to counteract the still-pervasive conditioning that tells women to play the "femininity" game. The femininity game says that even if you lose at every other game, you win the game if you win the man. Now any man that can only be won by a woman pretending she is something that she is not is no real man. He is a victim of the masculine mystique.

In prison, programs should not teach the femininity game or teach women to seduce men, for then they become victimized by it and fall back into the same vicious cycle. For some women, going to jail means that they are out of one jail (psychological jail for many women if they have been limited in their roles and opportunities) and into another. Let us seek to liberate the so-called "feminine" in men and to liberate the so-called "masculine" (the positive aspects) in women. Then we may begin to develop more fully human and humane people, and produce less authoritarian systems of correction as well. What we are working for is a kind of world where the power of love can begin to exceed the love of power.

THE CURRENT STATUS OF WOMEN IN PRISONS

MARTHA WHEELER
Past President, American Correctional Association
Ohio Department of Corrections

I think a lot about the criminal justice system as it deals with women, having been in corrections for almost as long as I can remember. The peak of my expertise in corrections was in my first six months as an adult employee, and it was all downhill after that; the longer I live and the more I work, the less I am positive about anything. But one of the things that has caused me some concern about the criminal justice system as it deals with women is something I'm sure you've encountered— that nobody seems to know a whole lot about what goes on with women, and if they do they don't write it down. Those of us who work in this area, and who have done so for any length of time, must plead guilty. We have been remiss in that we have not done more reporting or describing of our feelings and our observations, or indeed our recommendations. And because those of us who have been involved with women in the criminal justice system have done so little reporting, we have been victims of other people's reports.

Certain kinds of things have been reported which really relate only to men, and they have been said and heard and interpreted as though they also apply to women. There are some ways in which we need to set the records straight. For example, popular media report about massive institutions dealing with great quantities of men who are depersonalized, who are known only by last name or number. This tends to be heard as the description of correctional institutions totally, but women's institutions typically do not fit this description. I work with a total population of approximately 270. The state of Ohio operates one of the five largest state institutions for women. There are greater numbers in the federal institution in Alderson, West Virginia, and in New York, California, Texas, and North Carolina. Perhaps there are a few others that occasionally outnumber us, but most of the state institutions for women have populations between somewhere under fifty and about 300. This is scarcely a massive seething group of humanity.

We also have this picture of the depersonalized con, known only by last name and number, if indeed even that. In women's institutions, it is typical that there are several staff members who know a woman's whole name—maybe even her right name—and how many children she has and who is taking care of them. The whole picture of impersonality and enormousness simply does not describe facilities for women.

We also hear that the recidivism rate is around 65%. I doubt that this figure accurately reflects women. Most women in the Ohio institution are Ohioans, and they come to the institution having been sentenced by Ohio courts. Few of them are transients just passing through. Most of the women who are released from our institution are released to a program in Ohio and, in general, they plan to remain in Ohio. Should these women seriously offend again, they would probably reappear in the population in the Ohio Reformatory for Women. Over the last several years our statistics indicate that somewhere between 82% and 90% of our admissions are people we have never seen before. As of the calendar year 1972, about 88% of our admissions were new to our institution.

Now this is not necessarily to say that we are successful with women. I am simply pointing out that we have failed in our responsibility to report the situation, if it is indeed different from the situation as it exists for men. Women in our institutions

tend to believe what they read about prisons for men. They
tend to believe that prisons for women are also huge,
depersonalized places and that people recidivate at the rate of
65% and so forth. They see that it's not true here, but are
convinced that it's true everywhere else, and this reinforces
their feelings of probable failure. This expectation of failure and
fear of rejection is difficult for the staff to counteract.

We don't really know what the size of the "problem" is as it
relates to women in the criminal justice system. Women
constitute between 3% and 4% of the incarcerated population,
throughout the state and the federal systems, and yet women
constitute a little over half the total population of this country.
There exist a lot of form-fitting explanations, but none of them
totally satisfies me. I like to think that women are generally less
criminal in their behavior. I also like to think that perhaps
society is willing to deal in less punitive ways with women who
have been introduced into the criminal justice system. There are
probably a good many reasons why women are represented in
such small numbers in the incarcerated population. I don't
think anybody knows exactly why—or even how many women
are really involved with the criminal justice system.

Let us consider the entrance to the system to be contact with
law enforcement agencies, that is, arrest. I don't know to what
extent law enforcement agencies deal with women who are
involved with criminal behavior. It's a very frustrating thing to
try to find out. In connection with one of our projects, we are
attempting to discover how many women become the object of
concern by law enforcement agencies in a city in Ohio, and
we're having a good deal of difficulty extracting this information from the records of police agencies. I suspect this is largely
due to the fact that inadequate records are a common problem.
One state in this country monthly puts out beautifully bound
statistical reports about their state-operated corrections system,
but they do not separate their statistics according to sex. So, I
have no way of knowing which of these statistics refer to men
and which to women. We really need to know the size of the
problem, the nature of the behavior activity as it affects women

in the criminal justice system, the needs and the facilities, and the data must be made available to assess the problem.

The criminal justice system has its impact on any individual who becomes involved with it. It has a special impact on women. Some of them can be regarded as favorable impacts in that the system seems to be more forgiving toward women. It seems to be more tolerant of deviant behavior, for longer, from women than it is for men before imprisonment results; this perhaps accounts for some of the difference between 97% and 3%. For example, if a woman kills somebody, the chances are pretty good she will be locked up for a long period of time. On the other hand, women really have to do certain other kinds of offenses repeatedly before the court says, "That's enough; we will not tolerate any more and you are going to be locked up." So my perception is that the community loses patience with men before it loses patience with women, and to this extent we act perhaps to the women's advantage.

You are all aware that law enforcement agencies are largely male—prosecutors are mostly male, judges are mostly male—and the attitudes are inclined to be that gentle woman could not possibly have been involved in this behavior. So women are less likely to be suspected if crimes are committed, and they're less likely to be detected. They are perhaps less likely to be arrested and more likely to be the beneficiaries of excuses—it's some man's fault, or she got in with the wrong people. Women have a good many more escape hatches and receive a good deal more forgiving.

Other impacts different for women than for men are that the community generally is less frightened of women offenders, and women seem to be rejected by their families less than men. By the time men begin to come into the reformatory institution, they have begun to lose family support. By the time they get into the maximum security male institution, especially if they are multiple offenders, they may have lost most of their family and friends. This does not happen nearly as severely with women. The families of women are more likely to say, "She's still our daughter and we love her and she just got in with the wrong people and we're with her and she can come back to us."

Because facilities are small, there have been more opportunities for higher impact programs for women. From the point of view of the administrators of facilities for women, there are some favorable impacts, in that we have been permitted to be more innovative in some of our programs. This is not an unmixed blessing. To some extent we have been permitted to design and experiment and work with different kinds of programs. But, because systems largely are administered and funded and designed by and for men, male directors and the commissioners have not been concerned with controlling programs for women and have stated, "I don't know anything about women. You design the programs and you develop the agency. If we can be of any help to you, let us know." And so in a way, this has been a bit of a boon to those of us who wish to develop programs.

On the other hand, maybe the worst thing that has happened to us in terms of working with women is also related to the fact that we are so small in number in comparison with the male offender. We get forgotten in the planning of the total system. When people fight to invent programs for a system, they forget women. When they get ready to dole out funds, women are ignored. Because we are small in number, our facilities are small and the varity of programs is limited.

Even so, we probably have too many women locked up, and far too many men. They are locked up for reasons that, if we pursue them far enough, turn out to be punitive, vengeful. They have very little to do with necessity for protecting society, or even the necessity of improving their performance to make them more acceptable individuals. Because we are not entirely happy with locking people up, we begin to invent ways to add programs to make the lock-up seem more comfortable for those who are confined, and so more palatable for those who impose it. These refinements have been designed particularly for male facilities; they aren't necessarily either applicable or desirable for female facilities.

Vocational training and preparation for employment are concerns of many critics of the criminal justice system in relation to women, but some of our women are not career-minded, and they do not really have it in mind to go out and get a job and be self-supporting. Sometimes we think we are being very progressive by giving people opportunities to do what they want to do, but we have a tendency to make up their minds for them about what it is that they want to do. We take it for granted that they are oriented toward losing the traditional role of women, moving out into the work force, and reaching fulfillment of self and so forth. But when they talk to us, they describe themselves with very traditional views. A while back, one of our parole officers said, "We parole officers are out here saying to parolees, 'when are you going to get a job?' and their families are saying to them, 'when are you going to get a man?' and the parolee herself is thinking, 'when am I going to get a man?'."

The question, of course, is: Is it our responsibility to work with the woman on finding a whole new role, a whole new view of herself? Or is it our responsibility to meet her where she is and help her with programs which secure her where she is to deal more effectively, more productively, and hopefully more happily with the world that she's going to? At the risk of contradicting NOW,[1] I really have to say that we should let our women say something about where they are and where they want to be and where they want to go. If I feel that where they should be going is in terms of careers, then I may be imposing my values on them. We can't impose our standards, nor can we impose our views of lifestyles or our preferred world. I think that we have to deal with our people where they are.

In conclusion, if there is anything good about correctional institutions, there are some good things about women's institutions. Some of the good things are the fact that they are small, are often well staffed, and they have opportunities for interpersonal relationships in one-to-one situations. I've always been grateful that these conditions exist for women as a benefit of men's attitudes toward women. But institutions are not the preferred answer for women any more than they are for men. If we are to really make some desirable impacts on women in corrections, we need to emphasize development of alternatives to institutionalization rather than focusing wholly on improvement of the present facilities.

NOTE

1. National Organization for Women.

REMEDIES FOR WRONGS
Updating Programs for
Delinquent Girls

EILEEN N. SLACK
Alabama Youth Services
Chalkville Campus

Among the hundred girls who live with me on the campus of the Alabama State Training School for Girls in Chalkville, and among the hundreds of young persons with problems (not problem children) with whom I have worked for more than twenty years, most have had worse things done to them than they will ever do to anyone else. For the most part adult evils and frustrations have been lowered with vengence upon them. Many of the young women at the state school have had more fearful experiences and have faced more rejection by their eighteenth birthday than each of us will ever know in our entire lives. Because of this, these young adults often are filled with self-hatred and feel worthless; they have indeed been pushed beyond their thresholds of control and they act accordingly. Many young women at our state training school are trying to get the staff and other girls to reject them as most other adults and peers have done in the past.

Behind the words of a girl who shouts into my office, "I hate you, Dr. Slack. You make me sick"; behind the punch I receive now and again in my side when one of them is trying to make a point; behind a girl's hostility, adult-hating mannerisms, sullenness, and her tough broad swagger, there exist more indications of sincerity, more real strengths, more adaptability and survival mechanisms than we give her credit for. One can't help wonder how this young woman has learned to cope as well as she has in an environment which seems to elicit failure and the destruction of the individual.

In working with young adults, we must be realistic and alert to the wrongs which have affected these students, and we have to be candid about our problems and our shortcomings in helping them.

But the question persists; it arises again and again. How can any of us go about the job of reaching out to these youths? And this doesn't mean working with them through the old medical-model approach which views a girl as a sick person who might get better if she takes our prescription of treatment willingly and is then very grateful for what we have done. There is more to treatment than this—more variables than that old medical model—more things which influence the rehabilitation of young people. For one thing, the quality of the total milieu on a campus counts, and it is in the quality of interpersonal relationships within that milieu where the real values lie—where the new life-giving forces can be felt—both for students and staff

In a milieu or within the limited environment on a campus of a training school for youth, there is the need to stress the importance of consistency and caring for each and every young woman, all this within an aura of stability and support. This work can't be done with a staff that is content to settle for a quiet eight-hour tour of duty, watching these young women instead of working with them. Creating an environment where people care for one another and grow up and grow forth in it is difficult. This caring environment will not be created by those of us on the staff who walk around clutching our framed credentials, protecting our forty-hour, Monday to Friday, work-week. It will not be created by those of us who go about seeking to reinforce our shaky identities in so many rigid ways which show these young women on our campus that we are inflexible rather than involved.

Let me share some crude examples of what the above really means. I wave back to girls who wave in to me while I sit at my desk; I call back my hello to them, even when important bureaucratic visitors are with me; I invite them into the office to greet our guests. I may stand up and hug a girl who has come in just for that. I make myself do these things even when I can feel the tensions in me rise when I'm interrupted. But I take the time because it matters. On visiting day those girls who have no company (35-40) come up to the superintendent's cottage where my husband and I spend the two hours with them. He and I also attend and participate in the Sunday school program each Sunday at 10:30 in the morning although the Billy Graham or Norman Vincent Peale messages are not exactly what we would voluntarily select for ourselves. We do it to share with them and participate with them in their programs, and give them an example of a man and woman who love each other—and are making it together. It is my contention that an institution such as the state training school for girls needs firm encouragement from the top to create a caring environment both through constructive programming and individual self-involvement.

The tendency on the part of a superintendent is to make infants of the staff rather than give them responsibility and decision-making powers in concert with these young women to create an involved and a caring environment. Too often the tremendous pressures upon the superintendent are to make the staff help her achieve tranquility on the campus rather than treatment. Maturity in oneself, caring about others, respect for others, comes from an assumption of responsibility that allows one to do both of these things: to mature and to care. This growing up has to be accomplished in the lives of the staff, the young women in their care, and especially in the superintendent. Learning how to cope and how to care is fostered through individual decision-making. If a staff and the young people under their care are relieved of most campus responsibilities except the responsibility to adjust and conform, it is no surprise that both the staff and the girls are ill-prepared to decide things in their own minds when faced with difficulties. This includes such things as the girl who is lost when she returns home to alcoholic parents, or the staff member who cannot move ahead or press on when a superintendent is not on campus or an immediate superior is not available.

The stifling and harnessing of the human mind and the human heart can occur subtly, but are just as definite and just as insidious over a long period of time as with an immediate formal lock-up procedure. This harnessing of the human mind and heart occurs basically because the top authority figures in the institution are not willing to share their authority. When your authority is shared with someone, it says to that staff member that you respect her or him. You have confidence in that person's abilities.

All of us who work in the field of corrections are aware that authority, or what is sometimes more crudely referred to as "power" in correctional institutions, is not readily shared. For one thing, correctional institutions are often patterned after another model, not medical, but a military model with strata of authority arranged in such a way that the superintendent or warden, at the top, has an absolute say-so about matters in much the same way as the general in the army or the captain of the ship or president of the corporation. Let me add that I am not deluded into thinking that the word of the superintendent is really law or that the superintendent has real control of the power which is supposedly invested in the office. We are all too aware today of the fact that power is never what it seems. There are so many situations in which the person at the head of something has less control over things than the person at the bottom. Nevertheless, in most government institutions most of the time, the warden or the superintendent is the captain of the ship—the boat does not sail without her and, should it go down, she must sink with it. In this sense, the warden or superintendent does hold a certain authority or power within the institution and this power may be used for good or for evil, and effectively or ineffectively. It is the use of such power that I wish to focus on now in an effort to show how we can share power in order to update treatment programs for juveniles.

There are four strategic points for shared authority with staff and teenagers for the updating of treatment programs for a correctional institution. The first point is that authority must be shared from the top down. This means that from the warden or superintendent on down, power (and accompanying responsibility) must be delegated. This delegation must not exclude the young inmate who should be given as much power over her own life and that of other inmates as she can effectively use for rehabilitation. Examples are home furloughs, or Christmas shopping without institutional supervision.

The second point is that, although it is hard work to share authority, when it is shared properly nothing is lost. That is, when one person gives another person the freedom to decide what is best for herself, the first person does not really lose anything. Power is not surrendered just because it is shared.

Third, authority can never be actually shared in a general way. Authority must be made specific. It must be clear to everyone what authority or power, what decisions over what resources, what functions, and so on are being given to whom, for what purpose, with what consequences, with what means of looking at the outcomes . . . and for what period of time. Think for a minute about a program of community recreation—girls from a state training school bowling in a local center or swimming in a local YWCA. Whose responsibility is it?

The sharing of power or authority in a correctional institution does not mean the rule of laissez faire or everybody doing what she or he pleases all the time. It means instead the specific delegation of specific freedoms, authorities, and responsibilities to specific individuals or groups for specific periods of time. An obvious example is the following: it would be impossible to allow every young person and every staff member to smoke cigarettes in an institution anytime and anywhere. Fire laws would be violated and serious harm might come to many. However, it is possible to allow a group of young persons to decide on smoking rules within the institution for themselves and for specific periods of time as long as the means for looking at the outcome of their decisions and programs is also specified and clear to all. About six months ago our institution never allowed smoking for anyone. Now a fact sheet is studied by each girl on the hazards of smoking. She is then tested. If she passes it, she smokes. If she fails the test, she studies the fact sheet again and is tested again. This program is worked through campus council, composed of student-elected representatives from the student body. Smoking breaks are frequent but regulated as to areas.

The last point is that for a staff member to accept the concept of shared authority, the receiver must be able to identify positively with the giver. The receiver of the new authority must be convinced that the person giving the authority does so in the best interests of all and with positive motives, not just out of laziness or lack of concern or unwillingness to accept responsibility herself. Very often in institutions—especially those with teenagers as clients—the idea of punitive authority or punishment on the part of the staff is viewed by the teenager as synonymous with staff interest, concern, and even a substitute for the parental love the child misses so badly. Thus, as you try to create an atmosphere of freedom, freedom is hard to take; the young detainee is likely to feel that when she is left up to her own devices, nobody cares about her. For this reason, the authority figures within the institution must go to great lengths to establish this atmosphere of freedom and caring and to establish an "image" of concern for each individual within the institution. Throughout our new programs at Chalkville, the girl now has more freedom to decide things, but the staff are really interested in what she decides. It is not that we wish to maintain forever a maternal-paternal position in relation to the teenager—it is just that we must reach the young woman where she "is at," and work from there, gradually increasing the amount of authority and responsibility which is shared with her.

In conclusion, in working with juveniles in a training school, we need a diversified set of program offerings with the shared authority concept. We need to rekindle and talk about our faith in the potential of the young people in our care, and those who take care of them. And, it has to come from the top down. Girls adjudicated to our schools have to assume some responsibility in programs that affect them so directly. In these same programs staff have to be turned loose, so that they are encouraged to develop a "we" feeling—a feeling that all of us fellow workers are involved in the treatment effort of changing delinquent-type attitudes and values.

AN EX-OFFENDER EVALUATES CORRECTIONAL PROGRAMMING FOR WOMEN

FARRIS LAWRENCE
Rehabilitation Research Foundation

Treatment in the correctional system has not been as effective as intended. The modern philosophy is that the criminal is sick and can be cured by certain treatment procedures and turned back into the society. But nobody has control over another person's attitudes. You can work with her all you want to, but real change in attitude comes from within an individual and it is a voluntary thing. There is nothing voluntary about going to prison; you are definitely drafted. Any change is going to have to come from within this person, and she has to make up her own mind. Treatment programs are wonderful, but they have not really produced the desired effects.

What is needed is a preparation for these people to be sent back into society so that they are entitled to their own life style, and so that they are prepared to deal with life as it is. They must know how to do something that they can be paid for doing, because it has come up time and again that we need money to do anything. We cannot operate without money no matter what the program is. And unless these women have the money to live a normal life style, going to work like everybody else, they are going to do something to get money. This vicious cycle goes on and on—out, and back in again—with no basic change in ability to survive any other way.

Most women are employable. Most women want a job. They would rather go back into society and work at some job that would pay them a weekly salary. But there are m any women who do not know how to do anything that can earn money. That is what we are lacking in correctional systems—steady vocational programs that will teach women something that they can do and be paid a decent salary for doing. We need to raise our educational level, because a fifth-grade graduate cannot get a job making any money. If you go to prison ten times and come out ten times and you still don't have an education, you are still not making any money.

The Tutwiler Prison for Women in Alabama is a representative case. It houses approximately 125 at any given time. An institution serving a population this small could easily establish a vocational program that would operate on an individual basis—a vocational and educational program in which every person can achieve something. Everybody can make some kind of progress. Every woman leaving Tutwiler should take some sort of marketable skill that will provide her with employment so that she can take care of herself and her family. The job barriers for ex-convicts are destructive, and most governments are very guilty of legislating jobs at state, local, and federal levels that will not accept an ex-convict. The government tells private industry, "Hire the ex-convict," just like it says, "Hire the vet." They do not practice what they preach.

The parolee and the ex-convict are placed back in society where the situation is discouraging. Not very much is being done in Alabama. That is the only system I know about. Other parts of the country may be very progressive, but vocational and other programs must be extended to reach all of us so that the ex-offender does not go to the street with built-in handicaps.

Another real problem facing the ex-offender is the community acceptance when she goes back into society. The entire thrust of rehabilitation up until now has been on changing the offender, but what we need in addition is to direct our efforts to changing the attitude of the community. We would like to reeducate the community to realize that people who go to prison and come back out are still people—rather than monsters with horns. The ex-convict paid her debt to society and now she is ready to work within the society and make some sort of contribution to the system. But without acceptance she gets bitter, and it does not take long for her to be right back where she started. There are needs for building or rebuilding solid ties between the offender, the community, and her family. In some cases there are families that reject the member who goes to prison, even to the point of moving away without notification. If help for them does not come from the community, from people who are aware of the situation and can do something, they are forgotten.

Women have special problems; they have their children. They have children who may have been taught while they were gone that "your mother is no good, she's not fit." When she returns this is the major problem that faces her, because her role as mother is the one in which she expects to be accepted. Prisons can do all of the rehabilitating, treating, educating, or correcting that an inmate can absorb, but if she is not accepted by her family the improvement is not going to have a lasting effect.

Society keeps the offender from the very tools and means needed to change her—successful participation in community activities. The key to successful return to society lies in combining the ready resources of the community with a working relationship with correctional agencies. Work release programs and home furloughs are examples of this. If a woman has been incarcerated for a long period of time, she has forgotten a lot of problems that are there. Furloughs or work release keep her in touch with reality.

While I was away the prices went up, but I didn't feel it. I had read about it, but it didn't mean anything to me. By going into the community on work release I saw that it was going to be a struggle. The world was not going to be waiting for me when I got out. An ex-convict needs a running start to jump in there, or she will not survive.

New institutions are being planned. Why prepare for something that can be eliminated? Building a prison is one of the most "constructive" things that you can do. But it is not needed. It perpetuates a problem—the bigger prisons you have, the more people will be sent through the court to be sentenced because there will be somewhere to put them.

Spending money to build a better prision is a waste of resources. I would estimate that 60% of the female inmate population could better profit from a realistic community setting with some form of economic guidance and more frequent access to family interaction. The halfway house is solution that makes more sense to me.

Women in American society have been taught to define themselves in terms of men and therefore depend on a male system. Women are by nature dependent. Our society teaches us that to be smart, we should depend upon men for whatever we need. But I believe independence is the answer. Social and coping skills, including family life, education, and consumer training, are necessary to prepare women to deal with society without reliance on a public welfare system or on a temporary male guardian (a new boyfriend, until he gets broke). Women in prison need to focus on self-definition, self-realization, self-appreciation, and self-sufficiency. As Helen Reddy says so meaningfully in her battle hymn of the liberated woman, "I am strong, I am invincible, I can do anything—I am Woman!"

PLANNING FOR THE FEMALE OFFENDER
Directions for the Future

ANNETTE M. BRODSKY
Department of Psychology
University of Alabama

There are various points of contact with the criminal justice system in which female offenders need to be considered as female as well as offenders. While some of the issues discussed here might also apply to men, their impact on women is potentially greater because of the circumstances of women in our society. Equal treatment under the law should be a goal for all members of society, but the equality of the treatment requires a close look at the antecedents and consequences that might differentially affect the sexes outside the criminal justice system. Ignoring the differences in needs of men and women who are currently in the correctional system only serves to discriminate further against women as a minority.

ENTRY INTO THE CORRECTIONAL SYSTEM

Although fewer women enter the criminal justice system than men, the percentage of increase in women offenders is rising

Author's Note: *This paper was drawn in part from the workshops of the Third Alabama Symposium on Justice and the Behavioral Sciences. The moderators who contributed to this summary: Robert Seals, Ruth Ann Lyman, William Chambers, Marianne Rosenzweig, and Gerry Pollard.*

(Howard and Howard, 1974). Many of the offenses for which women are incarcerated are not acts of violence or even interference with the property or rights of others. A prominent sentiment of criminal justice planners is that many selected crime categories can be eliminated as legal offenses. Prostitution, victimless sex crimes, alcoholism and drugs, and juvenile status offenses are among those that typically affect women and might be good candidates for legislative reconsideration.

While programs of alternatives to incarceration for female offenders are emerging (MacArthur, 1972), few novel, individual solutions to the complex problems of female offenders have been found by planners. Sometimes the use of available funds might be more wisely allocated directly to the client (e.g., for emergency family crises or routine family maintenance), rather than fitting the client into the closest, often inappropriate, agency program. In some cases, diversion from the criminal justice system entirely lets a natural corrective process occur in which the offense becomes alien to the woman's self-concept; this is opposed to the more typical process of incorporating the belief, "I am a failure and a criminal, so I might as well act like one."

Flexibility in uses of alternatives is especially important for women who deviate from their typical behavior out of confusion of new roles. As opportunities for women and awareness of their capabilities broaden, access to new avenues of criminal activity occurs simultaneously. Thus, the advantages of more independence in the work world also bring greater risk and responsibility for which many women are not prepared. Law enforcement personnel are changing their chivalrous attitudes toward women and will be more likely to treat women harshly who commit offenses—and to treat them with less guilt or discomfort than they have in the past. In studies of attitudes of penology and law enforcement students (Brodsky and Rosenzweig, 1974), equal lenience toward women and men was indicated, as opposed to previous data which suggest favoritism toward women.

Some problems that are specific to women are encountered at the beginning of the criminal justice process. Appreciation of these difficulties has led law enforcement personnel to be reluctant to detain women in the past. Many offenders have dependent children or relatives who must be cared for if the woman is not permitted to return home immediately. Various sources (Singer, 1973) suggest that 60% to 80% of women in prison have dependent children. While some programs are being developed to provide temporary arrangements (MacArthur, 1974), this problem is not generally receiving attention from the courts and correctional centers which created the problem. Thus, an increase in detention of women will exacerbate this problem if it is ignored.

Not all women entering the system are those succumbing to the multiple handicaps of being female, nonwhite, and sole providers for dependents. An increasing population is the young, white, militant drug offenders. Alabama's women's prison, among others, has seen a 50% rise in its population over the last few years, which represents largely an increase of this segment. The experiences of this group of offenders differ from those of the offenders to which correctional staff have been accustomed. We need to pay attention to the diverse facts of life of the high-risk populations from which the offenders come.

As the needs and characteristics of the population change, the programs available must keep pace. We may not like the fact that these women are filling the jails and prisons, but their presence cannot be wished away. Until diversionary procedures are realized, awareness of drug abuse treatment is an obligation of correctional personnel.

INSTITUTIONAL SETTINGS

When we fail to provide the opportunities for prevention of crime, and when a woman fails to benefit from the programs aimed at keeping her out of the criminal justice system, then an institutional setting may be necessary for the protection of the community. Even those women who may be dangerous to themselves or others, or who are not capable of living in free, uncontrolled settings, should not be seen as homogeneous.

Their needs differ as much as the needs of male prisoners differ in an institution. While females still represent a small minority of the institutionalized population of offenders, classifying them only as females, as opposed to categories by age, offense, or security risk, does not help their situation.

Male institutions, however, should not be used as a model for females. Small, local facilities are felt to be most adaptive. The ultimate goal of a prison should be to teach the offender to live a life oriented away from an institution. Thus, adaptation to a large institution is a negative factor, desirable only for those who would not be able to function later outside a maximum security setting.

The obvious need is for institutions to be near the woman's home community. The sources of opportunity for future jobs, living arrangements, child care, and communication with the family become less likely and less realistic as the inmate is further detached from the community to which she will eventually return. Previous studies (Giallombardo, 1966; Ward and Kassebaum, 1965; Burkhart, 1973) indicate that lack of family ties is a critical deprivation experience for women in prison, which contributes to much situational homosexuality and personal anxieties.

Stop-gap measures to alleviate these problems will not serve long-range plans to keep women out of institutions. For example, the use of conjugal visits would serve only as a "Band-Aid" to the overall problems that institutionalized inmates encounter with relationships to their families. The assurance of adequate communication with the outside community, including but not restricted to the family, is the greater and more important need that conjugal visits attempt to remedy.

Developing coed institutions is a solution that is becoming more acceptable. This permits women to relate to men as co-workers and as partners in social interactions. For most women, learning to relate to men in nonsexual ways is a more important need than learning to attract men sexually. There is one less free-world adjustment for the released female offender if the correctional institution itself is integrated. The often expressed concerns of possible sexual assaults are not a reason for segregating the sexes, when considered in the light that sexual assaults in single-sex institutions have not been successfully avoided. The availability of vocational and educational programs to women is more equally realized by sharing of facilities, particularly when the economics of providing training for a small group of women, separately, is the alternative.

Staffing of institutions is an area of much debate. Many correctional workers feel that if the facility cannot be integrated by sex of residents, at least the residents should have opportunities for interactions with males as staff and volunteers. Staff should also be more representative of the various age groups and races that make up the institutions' populations. Provisions for use of women ex-offenders who have "made it" in staff positions might be helpful as role models as well.

Qualifications of staff could be clarified in many settings. Licensing requirements of correctional mental health personnel, as an example, are extremely variable. Some positions have requirements that are insufficient, while others seem unrealistically high for their duties. Often female personnel are not given opportunities to work in male settings, and the administrative positions are generally filled by males in facilities for both sexes. Salaries offered to the correctional officers who work most closely with the inmates are often unrealistically low in terms of what we expect from them. If these individuals are to represent dedicated, caring, helping persons, as opposed to mechanical turnkeys, then it would follow that they need financial compensation for coming and staying. Correctional officers cannot be selected carefully if the salary level brings only those who do not qualify for better paying jobs.

Barriers to becoming independent are difficult to overcome while in an institutional setting. Many women are still being returned to society without any preparation—financially, educationally, or socially. Child care courses and identification and counseling of child abusers are partial remedies. There is also a need to counsel women to deal with the stresses of poor family relationships and with their dependencies on others, including passive agreement to compromise their own values and judgment in order to keep a man.

One concern is that programs that are superficial attempts at personal development may lead to expectations that are not realistic. Women who have never assumed the stereotyped feminine role of the American suburban housewife may see this image as a dream to achieve (Konopka, 1966). Programs that prepare women for any role they are unlikely to achieve, basing their expectation on "charm" courses, or inflated feedback on minor successes in academic courses, may well be doing a great disservice in the long run. The development of personal pride is laudable, but exaggerated importance of a program's success is damnable. Many counselors and personal development courses ignore the reality of what the typical female offender has to face out on the street. One of the greatest problems of women who leave prison is their false expectations about the outside world, as well as our false expectations of what our programs and treatment can achieve. Criteria for parole prediction and recidivism are still largely unknown (Pauze, 1972).

COMMUNITY ACCEPTANCE

Returning to the community after incarceration is a critical time for the female offender. An interaction of culture shock, preexisting personality problems, and system-induced adjustment problems is common. Females experience these problems differently than men. Employment possibilities are severely restricted with prejudice against them as ex-offenders, women, and unskilled or unlicensed in their institutional trade. Women appear to receive less postrelease help than men, but may well have more need for work-release and other after-care programs.

The transition from the institution to the community is aided if the institutional programs include involvement with the community. Permitting inmates to volunteer in the community, e.g., as helpers in hospitals or in libraries, is an interesting reversal of the more typical use of volunteers from the community to enter the institution. The use of "client boards" to govern and veto programs for offenders helps ensure that continuation of a project would be based at least partially on client needs and positive responses. One major problem this particular procedure also addresses is agency rivalry, in which programs become geared more toward protecting the agency's status, as opposed to analyzing their failures and improving their services for the greatest needs of the clients.

Recidivism does not represent an accurate reflection of the success or failure of an institutional program as much as it reflects the lack of control over what happens to the inmate after release. The lack of acceptance in the community is the most difficult problem for the correctional process with female offenders. We need to examine the ways of "selling" the community on programs throughout the correctional process.

Familiarity programs involving community members, agencies, and civic groups as first-hand participants will demonstrate the humanness of the offenders. Utilizing "typical" citizens makes the program more real. On the converse side, by encouraging ex-offenders to work as change agents and to publicize their efforts, they may serve as models for the community. Speaking to civic groups and support of social, religious, and public service community groups in terms of their time, energy, commitment, and funds are productive ways of getting personal involvement and meaningful contributions from community members. Opening institutions and correctional programs to wider visitation, encouraging media description of programs, and requesting task forces of professionals to consult from the community are other ways to make the community feel responsible.

Two cautions must be raised concerning community awareness. There is an unfortunate tendency of community decision makers to "cream off" the successful cases for the best programs and to bring in cases that would otherwise not be admitted to a correctional facility, in order for these individuals to "take advantage" of the most attractive programs. Acceptance of the community means acceptance of the failures and problem cases also.

The implications of the current feminist movement for women in corrections are becoming evident. Predominantly, the advocates of reform for female offenders have been women. This is reflected in the percentage of studies about female offenders by women, compared to the percentage of studies in corrections in general done by women. This concern for women by women may be seen as an awakening to the plight of women in all areas of social concern; more specifically, the women's movement has fostered a sense of empathy or "sisterhood" with women who are seen as outcasts from traditional feminine roles. Many movement women are beginning to swell the ranks of female offenders and thus change the character of the population in penal settings to a more militant, demanding group of younger, middle-class offenders who have expectations of treatment and programs that have not been available in the past. These "new" women offenders will help to articulate the need for long-overdue programs for all female offenders. As the first feminist movement of this century was responsible for the establishment of separate prisons for women, then the current feminist movement will be the impetus for their reform, and perhaps their demise.

CONCLUSIONS

The move toward community involvement, decriminalization of nonvictim offenses, and the attention to family and vocational needs of women are themes that repeat themselves when workers in corrections discuss the female offender. Some of the problems faced by women in corrections are part of the difficulty with corrections as a whole. As a minority, women have typically been among the last to benefit from penal reform. The possibility is that the special problems of women will continue to wait until general reforms for men have been implemented. Hopefully, the 1974 National Advisory Commission on Criminal Justice Standards and Goals will serve as a guide to workers in the criminal justice system by its recommendations that neither size of population, sex of the offender, nor sex of the staff member is to be used as a justification for ignoring or limiting access to programs or opportunities for which there is a definite need. And, if correctional planners tarry long in having this point brought home by their co-workers, the chances are high that a more alerted female population, within the system and without, will serve as an increasingly potent reminder.

REFERENCES

BRODSKY, A. M. and M. ROSENZWEIG (1974) Research on the Female Offender. University of Alabama Center for Correctional Psychology Report No. 10.
BURKHART, K. W. (1973) Women in Prison. Garden City, N.Y.: Doubleday.
GIALLOMBARDO, R. (1966) Society of Women: A Study of a Women's Prison. New York: John Wiley.
HOWARD, E. M. and J. L. HOWARD (1974) "Women in institutions: treatment in prisons and mental hospitals," pp. 357-382 in V. Franks and V. Bartle, Women in Therapy. New York: Brunner/Mazel.
KONOPKA, G. (1966) The Adolescent Girl in Conflict. Englewood Cliffs, N.J.: Prentice-Hall.
MACARTHUR, V. A. (1974) From Convict to Citizen. Washington, D.C.: Commission on Status of Women.
PAUZE, B. K. (1972) "Parole prediction in Iowa." Master's thesis. University of Iowa.
SINGER, L. R. (1973) "Women and the correctional process." Amer. Criminal Law Rev. 11, 2: 295-308.
VELIMESIS, M. L. (1969) "Criminal justice for the female offender." Amer. Assn. of Univ. Women J. (October): 13-16.
WARD, D. A. and G. C. KASSEBAUM (1965) Women's Prison: Sex and Social Structure. Chicago: Aldine.